MILTON'S SONNETS

MILTON'S SONNETS

EDITED BY

E. A. J. HONIGMANN

SENIOR LECTURER IN ENGLISH IN
THE UNIVERSITY OF GLASGOW

MACMILLAN
London · Melbourne · Toronto

ST MARTIN'S PRESS
New York
1966

MACMILLAN AND COMPANY LIMITED
Little Essex Street London WC 2
also Bombay Calcutta Madras Melbourne

THE MACMILLAN COMPANY OF CANADA LIMITED
70 Bond Street Toronto 2

ST MARTIN'S PRESS INC
175 Fifth Avenue New York NY 10010

Library of Congress catalog card no. 66–22494

PRINTED IN GREAT BRITAIN

CONTENTS

PREFACE   vii

ABBREVIATIONS   ix

SONNETS   1

GENERAL INTRODUCTION   29

  I   *Topicality*   31
  II   *Tradition*   39
  III   *Text*   54
  IV   *The Order of the Sonnets*   59
  V   *The Italian Sonnets*   76

COLLATION AND COMMENTARY   83

Sonnet I, 85; Sonnet II, 89; Sonnet III, 90; Canzone, 91; Sonnet IV, 92; Sonnet V, 93; Sonnet VI, 94; Sonnet VII, 95; Sonnet VIII, 101; Sonnet IX, 105; Sonnet X, 110; Sonnet XI, 113; Sonnet XII, 121; Sonnet XIII, 126; Sonnet XIV, 133; Sonnet XV, 138; Sonnet XVI, 144; Sonnet XVII, 152; Sonnet XVIII, 162; Sonnet XIX, 169; Sonnet XX, 177; Sonnet XXI, 181; Sonnet XXII, 186; Sonnet XXIII, 190; On the new forcers of Conscience, 195

INDEX   205

ERRATUM

Page 99, line 14. *For* to that same lot'. *read* to that same lot', or '... measure equal to that same lot'.

PREFACE

THE last really detailed study of Milton's sonnets, J. S. Smart's edition of 1921, though a work of superb scholarship, is now out of date. Scores of articles have been published in the last half-century modifying or overturning Smart's conclusions : the time has come to gather this new material together, to defend Smart where he can be defended, and to assess the value of later contributions.

No editor of Milton's sonnets can escape the influence of Smart. My debts will appear on almost every page of this volume : occasionally I disagree with him, but never without the consciousness of living dangerously. I have, in addition, a special regard for him since it has been my privilege, as a member of the English Department in which he was for many years Queen Margaret Lecturer, to use the very books, in the collection of seventeenth-century first editions in Glasgow University Library, from which he acquired his mastery of the period. (Some of them once belonged to Principal Robert Baillie, supposedly the 'Scotch what d'ye call' of the sonnet *On the new forcers of Conscience*.) As a tribute to Smart I have reprinted his prose translations of the Italian sonnets, by kind permission of the present copyright owners (Jackson, Son & Co., Glasgow).

In preparing this new edition of the sonnets I have kept in mind the needs of two different types of reader : on the one hand, the sixth-former or undergraduate, who requires detailed annotation to explain the poet's literary technique and his allusions ; and, on the other, the specialist, for whose benefit I put forward new interpretations and facts concerning some of the sonnets, and take issue with Milton scholars when I think their views mistaken. The first two sections of the Introduction, dealing with Topicality and Tradition, were written for the undergraduate rather than the specialist; the reverse is true of the two sections on Text and The Italian Sonnets. The section on The Order of the Sonnets will, I hope, interest both kinds of reader.

As an annotator I have chosen to err on the side of fullness. With the Italian sonnets, however, it seemed best to follow a different course. I included these poems because they form part of the series: as most readers will only look at them — or at their translations — to see how they fit into the series, and as I am not competent to discuss them minutely, I have kept annotation to the minimum.

It is a pleasure, finally, to thank two friends, Professor J. C. Bryce and Miss H. A. Buchan, who very kindly read my manuscript and made various most perceptive suggestions; and a third one, Mr. Philip Drew, and also my wife, for whose assistance as proof-readers I am deeply grateful.

E. A. J. H.

ABBREVIATIONS

THE customary abbreviations are employed for periodicals. Works frequently referred to are quoted by short title only : their full titles will be found in the list below.

Brooks and Hardy. *Poems of Mr. John Milton. The 1645 Edition with Essays in Analysis*, by Cleanth Brooks and John Edward Hardy. New York, 1951.

C.M. *The Works of John Milton* (The Columbia Edition of the Works of John Milton), edited by F. A. Patterson, etc. 18 vols. and 2 index vols. New York, 1931–40.

Darbishire, *Lives. The Early Lives of Milton*, edited by Helen Darbishire. London, 1932.

Darbishire, *Poetical Works. The Poetical Works of John Milton*, edited by Helen Darbishire. 2 vols. Oxford, 1952, 1955.

Fletcher, *Poetical Works. John Milton's Complete Poetical Works Reproduced in Photographic Facsimile*, edited by Harris F. Fletcher. 4 vols. Urbana, 1943–8.

French, *Life Records. The Life Records of John Milton*, edited by J. Milton French. 5 vols. New Brunswick, 1949–58.

Hanford, *Handbook. A Milton Handbook*, by James H. Hanford (4th ed.). New York, 1946.

Hanford, 'Milton's Sonnets'. 'The Arrangement and Dates of Milton's Sonnets', by James H. Hanford (in *Modern Philology* (1920–1), xviii. 475–83).

Hughes. *John Milton Complete Poems and Major Prose*, edited by Merritt Y. Hughes. New York, 1957.

Keightley. *The Poems of John Milton*, edited by Thomas Keightley. 2 vols. London, 1859.

Kelley, 'Milton's Later Sonnets'. 'Milton's Later Sonnets and the Cambridge Manuscript', by Maurice Kelley (in *Modern Philology* (1956–7), liv. 20–25).

Life Records. See French.

Lives. See Darbishire.

Masson, *Life.*   *The Life of John Milton*, by David Masson.   6 vols. and index vol.   London, 1859–94 (vol. 1 revised 1881).

Masson, *Poetical Works.*   *The Poetical Works of John Milton*, edited by David Masson.   3 vols.   London, 1890.

Moody.   *The Complete Poetical Works of John Milton*, edited by William V. Moody.   Boston, 1899.

Newton.   *Paradise Regain'd* . . . *and Poems Upon Several Occasions*, edited by Thomas Newton.   London, 1752.

Nicolson, *John Milton.*   *John Milton — A Reader's Guide*, by Marjorie H. Nicolson.   London, 1964.

O.E.D.   *The Oxford English Dictionary*, edited by Sir James A. H. Murray, *et al.*   13 vols.   Oxford, 1933.

Pattison.   *The Sonnets of John Milton*, edited by Mark Pattison.   1883.

Prince.   *The Italian Element in Milton's Verse*, by F. T. Prince.   Oxford, 1954.

Smart.   *The Sonnets of Milton*, edited by John S. Smart.   Glasgow, 1921.

Todd.   *The Poetical Works of John Milton*, edited by Henry J. Todd.   7 vols.   London, 1809.

Verity.   *Milton's Sonnets*, edited by A. W. Verity.   Cambridge (Pitt Press Series, n.d.).

Warton.   *Poems Upon Several Occasions* . . . *By John Milton*, edited by Thomas Warton.   London, 1791.

Quotations from Milton's poems (other than the Sonnets) are taken from the first editions. *Paradise Lost*, however, is cited from the second edition of 1674. *P.L.* stands for *Paradise Lost*, *P.R.* for *Paradise Regained*. Milton's prose is quoted from the first editions as reprinted in *C.M.*

Sixteenth- and seventeenth-century authors are generally quoted in old spelling : the few exceptions (Shakespeare and some sonneteers) will be readily apparent. Biblical quotations come from the Authorised Version.

THE SONNETS

I

O Nightingale, that on yon bloomy Spray
  Warbl'st at eeve, when all the Woods are still,
  Thou with fresh hope the Lovers heart dost fill,
  While the jolly hours lead on propitious *May*,
Thy liquid notes that close the eye of Day,
  First heard before the shallow Cuccoo's bill,
  Portend success in love ; O if *Jove*'s will
  Have linkt that amorous power to thy soft lay,
Now timely sing, ere the rude Bird of Hate
  Foretell my hopeles doom in som Grove ny :
  As thou from yeer to yeer hast sung too late
For my relief ; yet hadst no reason why :
  Whether the Muse, or Love call thee his mate,
  Both them I serve, and of their train am I.

II

Donna leggiadra, il cui bel nome honora

L'herbosa val di Rheno, e il nobil varco,

Ben è colui d'ogni valore scarco,

Qual tuo spirto gentil non innamora,

Che dolcemente mostrasi di fuora

De' suoi atti soavi giamai parco,

E i don', che son d'amor saette ed arco,

Là onde l'alta tua virtù s'infiora.

Quando tu vaga parli, o lieta canti

Che mover possa duro alpestre legno,

Guardi ciascun a gli occhi, ed a gli orecchi

L'entrata, chi di te si truova indegno ;

Gratia sola di sù gli vaglia, inanti

Che'l disio amoroso al cuor s'invecchi.

Bright lady, whose fair name honours the flowery vale of Reno and the famous ford, truly is he destitute of all worth that is not moved to love by thy gentle spirit; which sweetly reveals itself — bounteous in pleasant looks, and the gifts that are the arrows and bow of Love — there, where blooms thy lofty might. When thou speakest in beauty, or singest in joy, so that the trees of the mountains might be moved, let him who is unworthy of thee guard well the entrance of his eyes and ears. Only grace from above may help him, ere amorous longing lingers in his heart.[1]

[1] The translations are not found in the editions of 1645 and 1673 : they are by J. S. Smart.

III

Qual in colle aspro, a l'imbrunir di sera,

L'avezza giovinetta pastorella

Va bagnando l'herbetta strana e bella

Che mal si spande a disusata spera

Fuor di sua natía alma primavera,

Così Amor meco insù la lingua snella

Desta il fior novo di strania favella,

Mentre io di te, vezzosamente altera,

Canto, dal mio buon popol non inteso,

E'l bel Tamigi cangio col bel Arno.

Amor lo volse, ed io a l'altrui peso

Seppi ch'Amor cosa mai volse indarno.

Deh ! foss'il mio cuor lento e'l duro seno

A chi pianta dal ciel sì buon terreno.

As on a rugged hill, at twilight of evening, the youthful shepherdess, accustomed there, waters a strange and beauteous plant, that hardly spreads its leaves in the unfamiliar clime, far from its genial native spring; so Love quickens on my swift tongue the new flower of a foreign speech, as I sing of thee, sweet and noble lady, — not understood by my own good people, — and change the fair Thames for the fair Arno. Love willed it; and I knew at the cost of others that Love never willed aught in vain. Ah ! were but my slow heart and hard bosom as good a soil to Him who plants from Heaven!

CANZONE

Ridonsi donne e giovani amorosi

M'accostandosi attorno, e : Perche scrivi,

Perche tu scrivi in lingua ignota e strana

Verseggiando d'amor, e come t'osi ?

Dinne, se la tua speme sia mai vana,

E de' pensieri lo miglior t'arrivi.

Così mi van burlando.   Altri rivi

Altri lidi t'aspettan, ed altre onde

Nelle cui verdi sponde

Spuntati ad hor ad hor a la tua chioma

L'immortal guiderdon d'eterne frondi :

Perche alle spalle tue soverchia soma ?

Canzon, dirotti, e tu per me rispondi :

Dice mia Donna, e'l suo dir è il mio cuore,

Questa è lingua di cui si vanta Amore.

Amorous youths and maidens gather about me with mirth, and, 'Why dost thou write?' they ask, 'Why dost thou write in a strange and unknown tongue, making verses of love, and how dost thou dare? Tell us; that so thy hope may not be vain, and the best of thy wishes be fulfilled.' And thus they jest with me — 'Other streams, other banks await thee, and other waves, on whose green margin there sometimes grows, to crown thy head, the immortal guerdon of unfading leaves. Why place upon thy shoulders a superfluous load?'

Song, I will tell thee, and thou shalt answer for me. My lady says, and her words are my heart, — 'This is the language in which Love takes pride.'

IV

Diodati, e te'l dirò con maraviglia,

    Quel ritroso io ch'amor spreggiar soléa

    E de' suoi lacci spesso mi ridéa,

    Già caddi, ov'huom dabben talhor s'impiglia.

Nè treccie d'oro, nè guancia vermiglia

    M'abbaglian sì, ma sotto nova idea

    Pellegrina bellezza che'l cuor bea,

    Portamenti alti honesti, e nelle ciglia

Quel sereno fulgor d'amabil nero,

    Parole adorne di lingua più d'una,

    E'l cantar che di mezzo l'hemispero

Traviar ben può la faticosa Luna;

    E degli occhi suoi avventa sì gran fuoco

    Che l'incerar gli orecchi mi fia poco.

Diodati — and I shall tell it thee with wonder — my stubborn self, that was wont to despise Love and often laughed at his snares, has now fallen where sometimes an upright man is entangled. Neither tresses of gold nor rosy cheek beguiles me thus; but, under a new form, strange beauty charms my heart, manners that are lofty and modest, and in her gaze a calm radiance of gentle black, delightful speech in languages more than one, and singing that from the mid hemisphere might lure the labouring moon; and from her eyes there darts such fire that to close my ears would avail me but little.

V

Per certo i bei vostr'occhi, Donna mia,

　　Esser non può che non sian lo mio sole,

　　Sì mi percuoton forte, come ei suole

　　Per l'arene di Libia chi s'invia ;

Mentre un caldo vapor (nè senti' pria)

　　Da quel lato si spinge ove mi duole,

　　Che forse amanti nelle lor parole

　　Chiaman sospir ; io non so che si sia :

Parte rinchiusa, e turbida si cela

　　Scossomi il petto, e poi n'uscendo poco

　　Quivi d'attorno o s'agghiaccia, o s'ingiela ;

Ma quanto a gli occhi giunge a trovar loco

　　Tutte le notti a me suol far piovose

　　Finchè mia Alba rivien colma di rose.

In truth, Lady mine, it cannot be but that your fair eyes are my sun, for
they smite me as powerfully as he beats upon one who makes his way
through the Libyan sands; whilst a warm vapour, such as I never felt
before, rises from the side where my suffering is, which perhaps lovers
in their own language call sighs: I know not what it may be. Part
thereof, confined and troubled, is hid beneath my breast, and then, escaping
into the air, is frozen or congealed. But so much as rises to the eyes
makes every night a time of tears, until my Morn returns crowned with
roses.

VI

Giovane piano, e semplicetto amante,

    Poi che fuggir me stesso in dubbio sono,

    Madonna, a voi del mio cuor l'humil dono

    Farò divoto ; io certo a prove tante

L'hebbi fedele, intrepido, costante,

    Di pensieri leggiadro, accorto, e buono ;

    Quando rugge il gran mondo, e scocca il tuono,

    S'arma di se, e d'intero diamante,

Tanto del forse, e d'invidia sicuro,

    Di timori, e speranze al popol use,

    Quanto d'ingegno, e d'alto valor vago,

E di cetra sonora, e delle Muse ;

    Sol troverete in tal parte men duro

    Ove Amor mise l'insanabil ago.

Young, gentle and simple lover that I am, and in doubt how to fly from myself, to you, Lady, I will make in devotion the humble gift of my heart. In many trials I have known it faithful, dauntless and loyal ; fair, wise and good in its thoughts. When the great sky resounds and thunder roars, it arms itself with itself, as with complete adamant ; as heedless of chance and envy, of common hopes and fears, as it is covetous of genius and lofty worth, and of the sounding lyre and of the Muses. Only there will you find it less hard, where Love placed his incurable sting.

VII

How soon hath Time the suttle theef of youth,
 Stoln on his wing my three and twentith yeer !
 My hasting dayes flie on with full career,
 But my late spring no bud or blossom shew'th.
Perhaps my semblance might deceive the truth,
 That I to manhood am arriv'd so near,
 And inward ripenes doth much less appear,
 That som more timely-happy spirits indu'th.
Yet be it less or more, or soon or slow,
 It shall be still in strictest measure eev'n,
 To that same lot, however mean, or high,
Toward which Time leads me, and the will of Heav'n;
 All is, if I have grace to use it so,
 As ever in my great task-Masters eye.

VIII

Captain or Colonel, or Knight in Arms,
   Whose chance on these defenceless dores may sease,
   If deed of honour did thee ever please,
   Guard them, and him within protect from harms,
He can requite thee, for he knows the charms
   That call Fame on such gentle acts as these,
   And he can spred thy Name o're Lands and Seas,
   What ever clime the Suns bright circle warms.
Lift not thy spear against the Muses Bowre,
   The great *Emathian* Conqueror bid spare
   The house of *Pindarus*, when Temple and Towre
Went to the ground : And the repeated air
   Of sad *Electra*'s Poet had the power
   To save th'*Athenian* Walls from ruine bare.

IX

Lady that in the prime of earliest youth,
   Wisely hast shun'd the broad way and the green,
   And with those few art eminently seen,
   That labour up the Hill of heav'nly Truth,
The better part with *Mary*, and with *Ruth*,
   Chosen thou hast, and they that overween,
   And at thy growing vertues fret their spleen,
   No anger find in thee, but pity and ruth.
Thy care is fixt, and zealously attends
   To fill thy odorous Lamp with deeds of light,
   And Hope that reaps not shame.   Therefore be sure
Thou, when the Bridegroom with his feastfull friends
   Passes to bliss at the mid hour of night,
   Hast gain'd thy entrance, Virgin wise and pure.

X

Daughter to that good Earl, once President
   Of *Englands* Counsel, and her Treasury,
   Who liv'd in both, unstain'd with gold or fee,
   And left them both, more in himself content,
Till the sad breaking of that Parlament
   Broke him, as that dishonest victory
   At *Chaeronéa*, fatal to liberty
   Kill'd with report that Old man eloquent,
Though later born, then to have known the dayes
   Wherin your Father flourisht, yet by you
   Madam, me thinks I see him living yet ;
So well your words his noble vertues praise,
   That all both judge you to relate them true,
   And to possess them, Honour'd *Margaret*.

XI

I did but prompt the age to quit their cloggs
   By the known rules of antient libertie,
   When strait a barbarous noise environs me
   Of Owles and Cuckoes, Asses, Apes and Doggs.
As when those Hinds that were transform'd to Froggs
   Raild at *Latona's* twin-born progenie
   Which after held the Sun and Moon in fee.
   But this is got by casting Pearl to Hoggs ;
That bawle for freedom in their senceless mood,
   And still revolt when truth would set them free.
   Licence they mean when they cry libertie ;
For who loves that, must first be wise and good ;
   But from that mark how far they roave we see
   For all this wast of wealth, and loss of blood.

XII

A Book was writ of late call'd *Tetrachordon* ;

And wov'n close, both matter, form and stile ;

The Subject new : it walk'd the Town a while,

Numbring good intellects ; now seldom por'd on.

Cries the stall-reader, bless us ! what a word on

A title page is this ! and some in file

Stand spelling fals, while one might walk to Mile-

End Green. Why is it harder Sirs then Gordon,

Colkitto, or Macdonnel, or Galasp ?

Those rugged names to our like mouths grow sleek

That would have made *Quintilian* stare and gasp.

Thy age, like ours, O Soul of Sir *John Cheek*,

Hated not Learning wors then Toad or Asp ;

When thou taught'st *Cambridge*, and King *Edward* Greek.

XIII

Harry whose tuneful and well measur'd Song
   First taught our English Musick how to span
   Words with just note and accent, not to scan
   With *Midas* Ears, committing short and long ;
Thy worth and skill exempts thee from the throng,
   With praise enough for Envy to look wan ;
   To after-age thou shalt be writ the man,
   That with smooth aire couldst humor best our tongue.
Thou honour'st Verse, and Verse must lend her wing
   To honour thee, the Priest of *Phoebus* Quire
   That tun'st their happiest lines in Hymn, or Story.
Dante shall give Fame leave to set thee higher
   Then his *Casella*, whom he woo'd to sing
   Met in the milder shades of Purgatory.

XIV

When Faith and Love which parted from thee never,
   Had ripen'd thy just soul to dwell with God,
   Meekly thou didst resign this earthy load
   Of Death, call'd Life ; which us from Life doth sever.
Thy Works and Alms and all thy good Endeavour
   Staid not behind, nor in the grave were trod ;
   But as Faith pointed with her golden rod,
   Follow'd thee up to joy and bliss for ever.
Love led them on, and Faith who knew them best
   Thy hand-maids, clad them o're with purple beams
   And azure wings, that up they flew so drest,
And spake the truth of thee in glorious Theams
   Before the Judge, who thenceforth bid thee rest
   And drink thy fill of pure immortal streams.

XV

Fairfax, whose name in armes through *Europe* rings
   Filling each mouth with envy, or with praise,
   And all her jealous monarchs with amaze,
   And rumors loud, that daunt remotest kings,
Thy firm unshak'n vertue ever brings
   Victory home, though new rebellions raise
   Thir Hydra heads, and the fals North displaies
   Her brok'n league, to impe their serpent wings,
O yet a nobler task awaites thy hand ;
   For what can Warr, but endless warr still breed,
   Till Truth, and Right from Violence be freed,
And Public Faith cleard from the shamefull brand
   Of Public Fraud.   In vain doth Valour bleed
   While Avarice, and Rapine share the land.

XVI

Cromwell, our cheif of men, who through a cloud
    Not of warr onely, but detractions rude,
    Guided by faith and matchless Fortitude
    To peace and truth thy glorious way hast plough'd,
And on the neck of crowned Fortune proud
    Hast reard Gods Trophies and his work pursu'd,
    While *Darwen* stream with blood of Scotts imbru'd,
    And *Dunbarr* feild resounds thy praises loud,
And *Worsters* laureat wreath ; yet much remaines
    To conquer still ; peace hath her victories
    No less renownd then warr, new foes arise
Threatning to bind our soules with secular chaines :
    Helpe us to save free Conscience from the paw
    Of hireling wolves whose Gospell is their maw.

XVII

Vane, young in yeares, but in sage counsell old,

   Then whome a better Senatour nere held

   The helme of *Rome*, when gownes not armes repelld

   The feirce *Epeirot* and the *African* bold,

Whether to settle peace or to unfold

   The drift of hollow states, hard to be spelld,

   Then to advise how warr may best, upheld,

   Move by her two maine nerves, Iron and Gold

In all her equipage ; besides to know

   Both spirituall powre and civill, what each meanes

   What severs each thou'hast learnt, which few have don.

The bounds of either sword to thee wee ow.

   Therfore on thy firme hand religion leanes

   In peace, and reck'ns thee her eldest son.

XVIII

Avenge O Lord thy slaughter'd Saints, whose bones
  Lie scatter'd on the Alpine mountains cold,
  Ev'n them who kept thy truth so pure of old
  When all our Fathers worship't Stocks and Stones,
Forget not : in thy book record their groanes
  Who were thy Sheep and in their antient Fold
  Slayn by the bloody *Piemontese* that roll'd
  Mother with Infant down the Rocks.   Their moans
The Vales redoubl'd to the Hills, and they
  To Heav'n.   Their martyr'd blood and ashes sow
  O're all th'*Italian* fields where still doth sway
The triple Tyrant : that from these may grow
  A hunderd-fold, who having learnt thy way
  Early may fly the *Babylonian* wo.

XIX

When I consider how my light is spent,
   Ere half my days, in this dark world and wide,
   And that one Talent which is death to hide,
   Lodg'd with me useless, though my Soul more bent
To serve therewith my Maker, and present
   My true account, least he returning chide,
   Doth God exact day-labour, light deny'd,
   I fondly ask ; But patience to prevent
That murmur, soon replies, God doth not need
   Either man's work or his own gifts, who best
   Bear his milde yoak, they serve him best, his State
Is Kingly. Thousands at his bidding speed
   And post o're Land and Ocean without rest :
   They also serve who only stand and waite.

XX

Lawrence of vertuous Father vertuous Son,
  Now that the Fields are dank, and ways are mire,
  Where shall we sometimes meet, and by the fire
  Help wast a sullen day ; what may be won
From the hard Season gaining : time will run
  On smoother, till *Favonius* re-inspire
  The frozen earth ; and cloth in fresh attire
  The Lillie and Rose, that neither sow'd nor spun.
What neat repast shall feast us, light and choice,
  Of Attick tast, with Wine, whence we may rise
  To hear the Lute well toucht, or artfull voice
Warble immortal Notes and *Tuskan* Ayre ?
  He who of those delights can judge, and spare
  To interpose them oft, is not unwise.

XXI

Cyriack, whose Grandsire on the Royal Bench

    Of Brittish *Themis,* with no mean applause

    Pronounc't and in his volumes taught our Lawes,

    Which others at their Barr so often wrench ;

To day deep thoughts resolve with me to drench

    In mirth, that after no repenting drawes ;

    Let *Euclid* rest and *Archimedes* pause,

    And what the *Swede* intend, and what the *French.*

To measure life, learn thou betimes, and know

    Toward solid good what leads the nearest way ;

    For other things mild Heav'n a time ordains,

And disapproves that care, though wise in show,

    That with superfluous burden loads the day,

    And when God sends a cheerful hour, refrains.

XXII

Cyriack, this three years day these eys, though clear
    To outward view, of blemish or of spot ;
    Bereft of light thir seeing have forgot,
    Nor to thir idle orbs doth sight appear
Of Sun or Moon or Starre throughout the year,
    Or man or woman.   Yet I argue not
    Against heavns hand or will, nor bate a jot
    Of heart or hope ; but still bear vp and steer
Right onward.   What supports me dost thou ask ?
    The conscience, Friend, to have lost them overply'd
    In libertyes defence, my noble task,
Of which all *Europe* talks from side to side.
    This thought might lead me through the worlds vain
        mask
    Content though blind, had I no better guide.

XXIII

Methought I saw my late espoused Saint
  Brought to me like *Alcestis* from the grave,
  Whom *Joves* great Son to her glad Husband gave,
  Rescu'd from death by force though pale and faint.
Mine as whom washt from spot of child-bed taint,
  Purification in the old Law did save,
  And such, as yet once more I trust to have
  Full sight of her in Heaven without restraint,
Came vested all in white, pure as her mind :
  Her face was vail'd, yet to my fancied sight,
  Love, sweetness, goodness, in her person shin'd
So clear, as in no face with more delight.
  But O as to embrace me she enclin'd
  I wak'd, she fled, and day brought back my night.

On the new forcers of Conscience
under the Long PARLIAMENT.

Because you have thrown of your Prelate Lord,
    And with stiff Vowes renounc'd his Liturgie
    To seise the widdow'd whore Pluralitie
    From them whose sin ye envi'd, not abhor'd,
Dare ye for this adjure the Civill Sword
    To force our Consciences that Christ set free,
    And ride us with a classic Hierarchy
    Taught ye by meer *A. S.* and *Rotherford* ?
Men whose Life, Learning, Faith and pure intent
    Would have been held in high esteem with *Paul*
    Must now be nam'd and printed Hereticks
By shallow *Edwards* and Scotch what d'ye call :
    But we do hope to find out all your tricks,
    Your plots and packing wors then those of *Trent*,
                That so the Parliament
May with their wholsom and preventive Shears
Clip your Phylacteries, though bauk your Ears,
                And succour our just Fears
When they shall read this clearly in your charge
New Presbyter is but *Old Priest* writ Large.

GENERAL
INTRODUCTION

I. TOPICALITY

IN almost every book on Milton it is repeated that his sonnets were 'occasional' poems. Enough is known about the date and background of individual sonnets to justify this attitude, yet after Masson's six-volume study of the poet's life, narrated, very properly, 'in connexion with the political, ecclesiastical, and literary history of his time', only J. S. Smart, in his splendid edition of 1921, thought it necessary to reinvestigate Milton's 'occasions', both public and private, on a fitting scale. Others, in the last forty-five years, have added new crumbs of information, which it will be useful to bring together in one volume: but no one seems to have had an idea of the riches still to be discovered, and of their possible effect on the interpretation of some of Milton's best poems.

The point may be illustrated very briefly. (i) Whilst the occasion of Milton's most magnificent sonnet, *Avenge O Lord* (XVIII), is now familiar to all the world, no commentator has noticed the verbal inspiration of so many 'Miltonic' lines and images in the news-letter accounts printed and reprinted in London within a few weeks of the Piedmontese atrocities. (ii) Neither Milton's editors nor, indeed, the *Oxford English Dictionary* give any help with a crucial allusion in the sonnet to Fairfax (XV) to 'the Public Faith', though the indexes of the *Journals of the House of Commons*, not to mention passing references in dozens of contemporary pamphlets, should have settled the difficulty. (iii) The only gloss to have appeared on Milton's allusion to 'Peace and Truth' in the sonnet to Cromwell (XVI) notes that

these words are found on coins issued by Parliament to commemorate Cromwell's victories.   Here the editor scented the
allusion, but failed to track it home.   For 'Peace and Truth' was
a catchphrase for the Covenant and, later, for the lost spirit of
the Covenant : so many authors signed themselves in the 1640's
and 1650's as 'a lover of Peace and Truth' that Milton's target
must have been larger than the Cromwell coins.

   Sonnet XI affords an even more revealing instance of the
elusiveness of Milton's 'occasions'.   The commentators inform
us that the distinction between liberty and licence, in 'Licence
they mean when they cry libertie', goes back to some famous
episodes in Roman history.   It is right that they should so inform
us, but, in addition, they ought to indicate that the *detraction* to
which Milton referred in his cancelled title for the sonnet flared
up against his divorce pamphlets, and that it was the battle-cry
of Milton's Presbyterian detractors that he and other 'sectaries'
were advocates of licentiousness rather than of true liberty.[1]
Milton, of course, emphasised in his works on divorce that he
stood for liberty and *not* for licence, but acknowledged that his
'profound accusers' brought against him 'the gross imputation
of broaching licence'.[2]

   Here, evidently, we are close to a personal issue in Milton's
sonnet much more important for its understanding than any
episodes in Roman history.   To get it into focus we must recall
that in November 1644, in the middle of his run of divorce

---

[1] '*Sectaries* . . . boast indeed (much) of the Spirit, but they manifestly doe
the workes of the flesh : They plead for libertie, but it is licentiousnesse . . .'
(John Ward, *God Iudging among the Gods* (1645), p. 26) ; 'It is well worthy of
your care to incourage . . . Liberty . . . God forbid, that any should expect
countenance from you, for any thing like *licentiousnes* . . .' (Thomas Hill, *The
Right Separation Incouraged* (1645) (preached 1644), A4ª) ; 'Why suffer ye . . .
uncleannesse and pollutions of marriage by maintaining a lawfulnesse of putting
away mens wives. . . . Why suffer ye books to be printed under colour of
maintaining liberty of conscience for the toleration of all sorts of heresies . . . ?'
(Francis Taylor, sermon preached 27 May 1646, p. 26).

[2] Cf. *Tetrachordon* and *The Judgment of Martin Bucer* (*C.M.* iv. 113, 14–20).

pamphlets, Milton published his *Areopagitica*. The stationers complained of this to the House of Lords :[1] Milton's sonnet-title, 'On the detraction which followed upon my writing certain treatises', may therefore refer to *Areopagitica* as well as the divorce pamphlets. We see then that Milton has contemptuously turned the licence-liberty catchphrase against his enemies, retorting upon them that much as they *bawle for freedom* they too may be said to believe in licence (the licensing of books), the very opposite of freedom in so far as it gags Truth (l. 10).

A poem much more widely discussed than the sonnets may further illustrate the dangers incurred by any critic heedless of the historical situation. 'How glad we are to escape from Eden', sighed Sir Walter Raleigh, '— we cannot settle down in the midst of this enormous bliss'.[2] Like other readers discomfited by Milton's factual descriptions in *Paradise Lost*, Book IV, Raleigh gave way to a post-Darwinian point of view, whereas the poet's contemporaries took their Paradise more seriously, debated its geographical location, studied its animal and vegetable population in bibles and scientific books, and, perhaps at the very time when Milton worked on Book IV, visited an exhibition modelling God's 'pleasant garden'.[3] Milton, we must suppose, looked upon his detailed survey as a special attraction.

Even the self-proclaimed historical critic sometimes fails to achieve a truly historical perspective. 'With Milton's contemporaries', Rajan decided, 'the response [to Satan] was predominantly one of fear.'[4] Theologians, of course, emphasised the

---

[1] Masson, *Life*, iii. 291 ff.   [2] *Milton* (n.d.), p. 121.

[3] *Paradise Transplanted* . . . Shown at Christopher Whiteheads at the two wreathed Posts in Shooe-Lane, London. Written by I. H. Gent. London . . . 1661. 'The Design, is a Model, or Representation of that Beautifull Prospect Adam had in Paradice. . . .' The author commends the artist's researches, his reproduction of all creatures 'from the greatest to the least, from the Elephant to the Mouse'. As Shoe Lane ran into Holborn, the exhibition was probably only minutes away from Milton's house.

[4] B. Rajan, *Paradise Lost and the Seventeenth Century Reader* (1947), p. 94.

fearfulness of Satan, but the 'common reader' was also acquainted with an extensive Lucifer literature of a coarsely humorous nature, typified by Nashe's *Pierce Peniless his Supplication to the Devil*: during the Civil Wars and in the years thereafter these pamphlets depicted a grimly sarcastic Lucifer who clearly left his mark on Milton's arch-fiend, being both 'the most high and mighty Emperor of Darkness', with all the poet's resounding titles, and an agreeable companion in depravity with a taste for heartiness and puns.

Not only is it easy to overlook Milton's topicalities (the editors of the sonnets were perhaps discouraged from further researches by the exemplary diligence of Masson and Smart), but it is also possible, as we have seen, to pick up an allusion but not all its implications, or to write too positively about a poem's 'occasion'. Perusing sonnet VIII (*Captain or Colonel*) we are bound to ask whether it presents us with a poetical situation or a practical expedient, and, if the former, whether the poet perhaps imagined the sonnet's little drama *after* 'the assault was intended to the city' rather than *before*: there are difficulties in each case, of which the reader must be warned, since his overall interpretation will be affected. Similarly it makes a difference whether sonnet XIX (*When I consider*) was composed in 1655, or three years earlier in 1652 when Milton became totally blind, or in 1644 when he first realised that his sight was threatened. An editor should identify the poet's 'occasions', but when necessary he should acknowledge that a poem may be variously interpreted.

One topical thread which runs through several sonnets (XI, XII, XV–XVII and *New Forcers*) may now be examined more closely. Milton's religious loyalties underwent so many changes that a reader could easily confuse the major parties, and even the poet's attitudes. As a young man, it will be remembered, Milton was an Anglican: he seems to have considered the ministry as a career, and certainly felt no special animosity towards bishops, two of whom he praised in Latin verses. Then, however, he came under the influence of Puritanism, reflected in *Lycidas* (1637) and, more violently, in his antiprelatical pamphlets (1641–1642). For a time he regarded himself as one of the Presbyterians, but his divorce-tracts (1643–5) brought him into disrepute with theirs, the stronger Parliamentary party (cf. p. 114), and so his sympathies were quite naturally engaged by the more tolerant Parliamentary minority, the Independents.

The battle between Presbyterians and Independents, glanced at in three of the sonnets (XI, XII and *New Forcers*), involved not only Parliament itself but also the Assembly of Divines, or Westminster Assembly (1643–9), called into being by Parliament to advise on a new church discipline and form of worship in place of the old episcopacy and Liturgy; and, inevitably, the argument was carried to the people in an endless stream of lively ephemeral pamphlets, as also in some immense and unreadable treatises.

As controversial pamphleteers the Independents held their own, but in Parliament, in the Assembly and in the country at large the Presbyterians greatly outnumbered them, and seemed likely to prevail. Moreover, the Scots threw all their weight behind the English Presbyterians: they signed the Solemn League and Covenant (1643) with the intention of imposing Presbyterianism on the three kingdoms, despatched an army southwards to aid their allies, and empowered eight Commissioners to treat with Parliament for the union of the Churches and to sit in the Westminster Assembly, there to guide the wayward English to the light. Three of the most forceful of these Commissioners are mentioned in the sonnets, by no means flatteringly: George Gillespie ('Galasp') in XII, and Robert Baillie ('Scotch what d'ye call') and Samuel Rutherfurd in *New Forcers*.

Having disposed of Anglicanism, the Presbyterians now in their turn desired an Established Church, to be modelled on that of

Scotland. It was proposed that England be divided into parishes or congregations, each in the charge of a minister and ruling elders: ten or twelve congregations would then form a Presbytery or *Classis* (cf. *New Forcers*, l. 7), the Presbyteries of a shire or ecclesiastical district meeting periodically in a Provincial Synod, representatives from which would go to an annual National Assembly. A *Directory for Public Worship*, replacing the old Liturgy, was to ensure uniformity throughout the new Church.

It soon became clear to the Independents in the Westminster Assembly that Presbyterianism was too strong for them. Their leaders, including William Bridge, Thomas Goodwin, Philip Nye and Sidrach Simpson (who re-enter the story of Milton's religious polemics in 1652) therefore pleaded for freedom of worship for independent congregations outside the Established Church. This the Presbyterians were unwilling to allow, being alarmed by the multiplication of sects, some of them in their view highly scandalous ones. They respected the Congregationalists or Orthodox Independents but not the Anabaptists, Brownists, Millenaries, Mortalists, etc., and they abominated some of the new 'heretics', such as the Divorcers, with whom Milton was popularly associated.[1] The sectaries, threatened with the loss of their newly acquired freedom, retorted that Presbyterianism no more than the Anglican and Roman Churches should 'force our Consciences that Christ set free' (*New Forcers*).

Outnumbered and divided amongst themselves, the Independents nevertheless predominated in one important department of the new state, and with its backing triumphed in the end. The 'New Model', i.e. the Parliamentary Army as reconstituted in 1645, was officered largely by Independents, one of whom, Oliver Cromwell, its presiding genius long before he became commander-in-chief in 1650, used all his momentous influence to resist intolerant Presbyterianism.

---

[1] For an account of the various sects in the 1640's cf. Masson, *Life*, iii. 136 ff.

The Presbyterians in the House of Commons recognised their danger, and tried to disband the Army in the lull (1646–8) between the two Civil Wars, in order to deprive Cromwell and his Independent officers of their source of power. But the Army refused to disband and instead marched on London (1647), causing the Presbyterian leaders in Parliament to flee the country. The Scottish Commissioners, all their hopes defeated, thereupon signed a secret treaty with Charles I, who promised to confirm the Covenant and Presbyterian Church government, and to suppress Independents of every sort (December 1647). From this treaty sprang the brief Second Civil War of 1648 : the Scots crossed the border once more, and various *new rebellions* by the Royalists raised their *Hydra heads* in support (sonnet XV). Cromwell and Fairfax dealt with these in the field — allowing the Presbyterians, meanwhile, to re-establish themselves in Parliament.

To settle their differences with this Parliamentary opposition once and for all, the Independents in the Army arrested or excluded 143 disaffected (Presbyterian) members, a *coup* now known as Pride's Purge, and proceeded to the trial of the king — 'illegalities' against which the Presbyterians loudly protested (December–January 1648–9).

After the king's execution (30 January 1649) Presbyterianism was kept in check at home as a political force. Scotland, however, continued to crusade for the Covenant, only to be crushed by Cromwell's Army of Sectaries at Dunbar (1650) and Worcester (1651).

Having seized control of the Long Parliament, a remnant of which survived until 1653 as 'the Rump', the Independents now governed the country and could plan more constructively for the future. To the horror of Milton and other extremist adherents, their own party began to contemplate the setting up of a National or Established Church. The very men who had fought against a Presbyterian Establishment in the Westminster Assembly,

Bridge, Goodwin, Nye and Simpson, in 1652 petitioned Parliament to make a settlement — though admittedly one more tolerant of dissenters. Milton's outburst against these *new foes* in the sonnet to Cromwell (XVI), and his sarcastic but more subdued reflections in the sonnet to Vane (XVII), reaffirm the hostility to *hirelings* and the *Civil Sword* expressed earlier in *New Forcers*.

There can be no doubt that Milton already at this time resented the implications in the ideas of Establishment and Dissent, and wished Christians of every kind to be free to organise themselves as they saw fit. Like other Tolerationists he insisted in the distinctness of *spirituall powre and civill* (XVII. 10), reducing the former, as Smart explained, to 'the control of each congregation over its own members, as it existed in the primitive Church'.

The guiding rule [Smart went on] was to be found in those Epistles where St. Paul instructs and admonishes the Christian converts; and the modern congregations, like those of the apostolic age, should govern themselves alone, asking no authority over others, and leaving the civil law to the civil magistrate, to be exercised in purely secular affairs (p. 96).

In short, Milton believed in 'voluntary association', which he expounded more fully in 1659, and he could justifiably claim that if he had changed parties he had not deviated from his principles, at least in so far as toleration was concerned. Consequently it is scarcely surprising that, having spent a decade in the bitterest opposition to the paw of the wolf (XVI. 13–14), he responded with such passionate fellow-feeling when the Piedmontese massacred a religious minority (XVIII).

This, then, is a rough outline of church affairs at the time of the sonnets, and of Milton's affiliations and attitudes. The story has its continuity, and is best told in a single sweep: but I have omitted much of the relevant detail, which will follow in the commentaries on individual sonnets.

II. TRADITION

WHILE the occasional or topical in Milton's sonnets still requires heavy annotation, most of his debts to the 'poetic tradition' are now common knowledge, and may be summarised quite rapidly.

The obscure origins of the sonnet, in the thirteenth or possibly the twelfth century, need not detain us. Suffice it to say that the form was known before it was taken up by Petrarch (1304–74), who chose it for his love-poetry and made it immensely popular. His example, and that of his Italian followers, stimulated poets in other European countries as these came under the spell of the Renaissance : the French *Pléiade*, in particular, cultivated the love-sonnet with great success.

Sir Thomas Wyatt (?1503–42) was apparently the first to introduce the sonnet in England, aided by Henry Howard, Earl of Surrey (?1517–47). After a period of neglect the poets of the 1580's and 1590's rediscovered it, and minor poets in their swarms turned out sonnet-cycles to Delia and Phillis, to Diella and Fidessa, to Chloris and Diana (Daniel, Lodge, R. L., Griffin, Smith and Constable). As earlier in Italy, every bright young man fell to sonneteering, a situation ridiculed by Ben Jonson in *Every Man in his Humour*, where the foolish Matheo boasts that he will 'write you your half score or your dozen of sonnets at a sitting'. A few more gifted poets also succumbed to the fashion — Sidney, Spenser (not here at his best) and Shakespeare.

The great fault of the Elizabethan sonnet was undoubtedly its easy flow, its all-too-manifest facility. Even Shakespeare, who could write in various styles, adopted the 'mellifluous and honey-tongued' manner in his 'sugared sonnets' (as Francis Meres put it in 1598), though in his case deceptively, for, unlike his contemporaries, he rarely inclines us to call for more matter with less art. When Milton in the middle of the seventeenth century gave new life to the form, which was now outmoded, his standards were totally different: instead of the verbal abundance and lusciousness of the past he preferred a classical restraint.

His allusions and syntax, as also the founding of certain sonnets upon Horatian precedents (cf. Index), reinforced this classicism. While we may suppose that Milton's general stylistic development — in prose as well as verse — would have made inevitable such a remodelling of the sonnet, it is worth remembering that the metaphysical poets also reacted against the older verbal luxuriance, and that Milton's sonnets, though not metaphysical or 'conceited',[1] therefore moved with the times.

But in order to understand Milton's place in the tradition we must turn back from the Elizabethan sonnet to the sixteenth-century Italians. As Smart and F. T. Prince have demonstrated, his most important teacher was Giovanni Della Casa (1503–56), who perfected the 'magnificent' style, the basis of the best of Milton's sonnets as of *Paradise Lost*. The secret of Della Casa's 'loftiness' lay, according to a near-contemporary admirer, 'in the wonderful skill he showed in breaking up the verses, and in separating the words which are commonly placed together'[2] — a secret penetrated by Milton and used to advantage.

[1] His Italian sonnets, however, have their full share of conceits.

[2] Cf. Prince, p. 21. Though their overall effect differs sharply from that of the 'magnificent' poets, the English metaphysicals also broke up verses and displaced words, and thus achieved the loftiness of, for example, Donne's *Holy Sonnets*:

> At the round earth's imagined corners, blow
> Your trumpets, angels, and arise, arise
> From death, your numberless infinities
> Of souls, and to your scattered bodies go,
> All whom the flood did and fire shall o'erthrow,
> All whom war, dearth, age, agues, tyrannies,
> Despair, law, chance, hath slain, and you whose eyes
> Shall behold God, and never taste death's woe. . . .

Della Casa emancipated the Italian sonnet from a framework that had become too rigid. Whereas Petrarch and his early imitators divided the sonnet into four parts, two quatrains (the octave) and two tercets (the sestet), and made the syntax dependent on these divisions, with a pause after each one, Della Casa dissociated syntax and metrics by means of *enjambement*.

Milton copied both Italian types, not infrequently tending towards the Petrarchan, or something very like it, when the subject demanded gracefulness (e.g. X, XIII and XIV), but preferring the method of Della Casa when he strove for the sublime (e.g. XVI, XVIII and XIX). Both gave play to characteristic Miltonic styles, practised by him in other poems over a large span of years. Using the latter, he made his words exert greater pressure upon one another:

Even in the Best Writers you Somtimes find Words and Sentences which hang on so Loosely you may Blow 'em off; *Milton's* are all Substance and Weight; Fewer would not have Serv'd the Turn, and More would have been Superfluous.[1]

'Facility' is the last charge one would bring against Milton's sonnets: their finely chiselled effects, resulting from much careful rephrasing, the signs of which abound in his manuscript, give, instead, an impression of keenly deliberated workmanship. Yet, whether he chooses the rigid scheme of Petrarch or the more flexible one of Della Casa, his sentences are always so perfectly articulated that to talk of their 'easy flow' would imply no self-contradiction. For all its involutions, sonnet XIX (*When I consider*) turns effortlessly on the simplest axis ('I ask: Patience replies'), and is at once intelligible: it differs in its fluency from the typical Elizabethan sonnet, which moves forward from point to point, in that it possesses a controlling centre.

[1] Jonathan Richardson, 1734 (*Lives*, p. 315). For a more modern and specialised discussion cf. Taylor Stoehr, 'Syntax and Poetic Form in Milton's Sonnets' (*English Studies* (1964), xlv. 289–301).

Milton not only replaced the verbal luxuriance of the Elizabethan sonnet with a classical precision, but he also abandoned
its formal structure.   The sonnets of Surrey and Shakespeare,
which represent the Elizabethan standard,[1] consisted of three
quatrains and a couplet, rhyming abab, cdcd, efef, gg.   Milton
returned to the Italian scheme of two quatrains and two tercets.
Like the Italians he employed only two rhymes in the octave
(abba, abba, *enclosed* rhyme, Milton's invariable choice — though
alternate rhyme, abab, abab, was also permitted).   In the sestet the
Italians gave more freedom, either two rhymes or three being
possible, with various combinations of each : eight different
arrangements are found in Milton's English sonnets, including one
with a final couplet (XVI) and one with a 'tail' (*New Forcers*).

In the purer Italian form, it need scarcely be said, the break
after the second quatrain is more strongly felt than in the Elizabethan variant : a new rhyme coming after the fourfold repetition
of two rhymes in eight lines has a more striking effect than one
following four different rhymes only twice repeated.   The Italian
form therefore encourages a syntactic pause or turn after the
octave, from which the whole poem may derive an internal
nexus.[2]

One of Smart's most notable achievements was his demolition
of what used to be called 'the Italian principle of the *volta*', to
which some nineteenth-century critics attached great importance.
A 'suspense or turn' after the two quatrains had been postulated
by Francis Hueffer, Watts-Dunton and others, making two separate paragraphs of the octave and sestet, the latter either presenting
the subject in a new light, or rejecting the octave's point of view

---

[1] A few Elizabethan poets did, however, experiment with the Italian scheme,
Constable, Sidney, etc. (Smart, p. 22).

[2] Shakespeare could of course have a *turn* in l. 9 (cf. No. 29 : 'When in dis-
grace with Fortune and men's eyes'), but his form invited the characteristic
twist in the final couplet (cf. No. 30 : 'When to the sessions of sweet silent
thought').

altogether : and Milton was censured for disregarding this 'rise and fall', this principle of principles in the sonnet. Smart, however, on checking the historical credentials of the *volta*, was able to show that the Italian critics never insisted on a *volta* or turn in the sonnet, and were misrepresented by Hueffer and Watts-Dunton : 'Milton cannot be reproached for disregarding the Italian principle of the *volta* in the sonnet; for there is no such principle.' At the same time Smart agreed that in Italian literature

it is doubtless possible to find many sonnets in which a marked pause in the sense occurs after the quatrains, and a certain change of theme, or the presentation of a fresh view of the subject, begins with the tercets (p. 36).

Whether or not Hueffer and Watts-Dunton misrepresented the Italian critics is, perhaps, of less moment than the fact that a pause or turn was employed by so many Italian sonneteers. It would not be wholly unjust, I think, to call it an 'Italian principle'. Whatever name we finally select, the frequency with which Milton placed a turn at the very commencement of the sestet proves that he understood the intentions of earlier poets (cf. VII, X, XIII, XV and XX). A sharp turn, less exactly coinciding with the start of the sestet, is also found elsewhere, in the eighth, ninth or tenth lines (XI, XVI, XVII, XIX and XXII), and confirms that a structural principle is involved — though not, be it added, one to which Milton felt invariably committed.[1]

I mention this central turn not only for its own sake but because of its connection with another device, the thought that turns back upon itself in the concluding lines. Sometimes this backward glance at the end is quite undisguised. In XVIII (*Avenge O*

[1] Smart (pp. 32–3) noted the 'sudden pause' in some of Milton's sonnets, and Prince (p. 92 ff.) wrote interestingly about their 'parallelism or duplex structure'. In an important review of Smart's book E. P. Kuhl drew attention to the 'full stop in the sense' in Italian sonnets after the octave, and to Wordsworth's anticipation of Hueffer and Watts-Dunton (*Modern Language Notes* (1924), xxxix. 45–50).

Lord) the bones *scatter'd* on the Alpine mountains cold have an
obvious relationship with the blood and ashes *sown* o'er all the
Italian fields, as has *thy truth* with *thy way*. The final words in
the first and last lines of XII (*A Book was writ of late*), i.e. *Tetrachordon* and *Greek*, similarly flash back and forth to one another.
But Milton may work more deviously. In XIX (*When I consider*)
the spaciousness of 'this dark world and wide' as experienced by
a single self-centred and restless man gives way to the vision of
thousands of God-centred angels posting 'o're Land and Ocean
without rest' — a deliberate contrast, but not as logically established as that between 'bent To *serve*' and 'They also *serve* who
only stand and waite'.

So, too, an implicit contrast or turn is found, I think, in the
backward glance of VII (*How soon hath Time*). Here the poet's
uneasiness about false appearances, in the octave, is cancelled by
the reflection that the *great task-Masters eye* sees *the truth*, so that
no mere *semblance* can *deceive*. The question sent to Lawrence
(XX) ('Where shall we *sometimes* meet ?'), is superseded when
the poem concludes with 'interpose them *oft*'. And the worldly
pleasures implied by *the broad way and the green* yield at the end
of IX (*Lady*) to the heavenly *bliss* of the *Bridegroom with his feastfull
friends*, a contrast reinforced by *the prime of earliest youth* and *the
mid hour of night*.

Again, the praise of Cyriack Skinner's *Grandsire* in XXI is not
simply a bow to a famous ancestor, a traditional courtesy in this
type of poem (cf. p. 48). It enables Milton to slip in the thought
that the misguided *wrench our laws*, from which he proceeds to
insinuate that Skinner wrenches life, overburdening it with cares :
the contrast between Coke, who interpreted *our Lawes* correctly,
and Skinner, who could not *measure life* correctly, is underlined
with *applause* for the one (first quatrain) and *Heaven's disapproval*
of the other (second tercet).

Perhaps the neatest reversal comes in XXIII (*Methought I saw*),

which opens with an emergence from darkness and closes with a
return to darkness, the wife '*Brought* [back] . . . from the *grave*'
to daylight, and the blind poet for whom day '*brought* back my
night'.

Though popularly associated with love-poetry, the sonnet, as
Smart emphasised, was by no means restricted to a single motive.
'Even Petrarch does not always speak of Laura.' One of Milton's
favourite poets, Tasso, divided his sonnets into three groups —
'Love Sonnets, of which there are 419; Heroical Sonnets, 486;
Sacred and Moral Sonnets, 87' — the second, poems of compliment and praise, being the model of those addressed by Milton
to Fairfax, Cromwell and Vane.[1] In addition the sonnet frequently gave utterance to feelings of friendship, and sometimes,

although much more rarely, to hostility and scorn. Addresses of
compliment to fellow-authors were composed . . . and on certain
occasions the sonnet supplied the purpose of a poetic epistle. It is
so used by Milton in the lines addressed to Lawrence and Skinner.

Milton, however, drew upon a larger 'tradition' than the
world of the sonnet. Like other writers of his day he shaped
every literary exercise, in prose and in verse, according to 'topics'
established by earlier practice. All of his sonnets fall unmistakably
into one or more of these categories, and it is therefore essential
to study them in this larger context — which may bring out
poetical intentions easily overlooked by the modern reader.

The important topics often embraced several subsidiaries.
Puttenham wrote of the *lamentation* that it could take as many
forms as there are sorrows.

Nowe are the causes of mans sorrowes many : the death of his parents,
frends . . . the desolations of countreis, the losse of goods and worldly
promotions, honour and good renowne : finally the trauails and tor-
ments of loue forlorne or ill bestowed.

[1] Smart, pp. 4, 40–41.

On this reckoning we can define as lamentations sonnets I and XXIII (love forlorn), XIV and XXIII (death of friends) and XVIII (desolation of countries), while others seem to start off as lamentations but change their course (VII, XIX and XXII).

On three occasions Milton composed a lamentation commemorating a person or persons deceased (XIV, XVIII and XXIII). There could scarcely be three more different poems, for each one draws on different conventions. *When Faith and Love* has affinities with the *epitaph*, and may well have been intended for, or inspired by, a tablet or monument placing Mrs Thomason between those two vividly realised personifications, the angels of Faith and Love.[1] Certainly the ideas and allusions derive from the epitaph, as these verses show:

> *On Charles Langley*; *St. Giles's, Cripplegate*, 1601.
>
> If Langley's life you list to know,
>   Read on and take a view;
> Of faith and hope I will not speak,
>   His works shall shew them true . . .
> Thus being dead, yet still he lives,
>   Lives never more to dye,
> In heaven's bliss, in world's fame,
>   And so I trust shall I.[2]

Like Milton, the poet speaks in commonplaces: he dwells on the exemplary life and good deeds of the deceased, affirms his confidence in resurrection, and echoes the biblical paradox that death brings true life; he alludes to faith and hope, as Milton does to Faith and Love, personifications found in various contemporary epitaphs and also represented in funeral sculptures.

---

[1] There was a monument for Mrs Thomason's grandfather in the church of St Dunstan's in the West, in Fleet Street, where Mrs Thomason herself was buried (cf. Smart, pp. 80, 164). Milton may have heard of a design to put up a monument for her, flanked by Faith and Love, and written his sonnet prematurely — just as he wrote some complimentary verses too early (cf. p. 49).

[2] *A Collection of Epitaphs and Monumental Inscriptions* (1806, 2 vols.), ii. 80.

With Milton's lamentation for his *late espoused Saint* (XXIII) the editors have compared other *visions*, such as Raleigh's '*Methought I saw* the grave where Laura lay'. Italian poets had anticipated Milton more closely, as in Berardino Rota's sonnet, a bereaved husband's dream of his dead wife:[1]

> In lieto e pien di riverenza aspetto,
> Con vesta di color bianco e vermiglio,
> Di doppia luce serenato il ciglio,
> Mi viene in sonno il mio dolce diletto.
> Io me l' inchino, e con cortese affetto
> Seco ragiono e seco mi consiglio,
> Com' abbia a governarmi in quest' esiglio;
> E piango intanto, e la risposta aspetto.
> Ella m' ascolta e fisa, e dice cose
> Veramente celesti, ed io l' apprendo,
> E serbo ancor nella memoria ascose.
> Mi lascia alfine, e parte, e va spargendo
> Per l' aria nel partir viole e rose:
> Io gli porgo la man, poi mi riprendo.

To the foreign models should be added other English ones, to stress the conventionality of Milton's 'occasional' poem: B. Griffin's dream of his lady (*Fidessa*, 1596, no. 14: 'With that, away she went: and I did wake withal . . .'), or W. Smith's (*Chloris*, 1596, no. 13: '*Methought I saw* the nymph I would embrace . . .'). Even more interesting is Sidney's (*Astrophel and Stella*, 1591, no. 38):

> This night, while sleep begins with heavy wings
> To hatch mine eyes, and that unbitted thought
> Doth fall to stray, and my chief powers are brought
> To leave the sceptre of all subject things,
> The first that straight my fancy's error brings
> Unto my mind, is Stella's image, wrought
> By Love's own self, but with so curious draught
> That she, methinks, not only shines but sings.

[1] Cf. Todd, 496–9; Smart, 125; and also T. B. Stroup, 'Aeneas' Vision of Creusa and Milton's Twenty-Third Sonnet' (*P.Q.* (1960), xxxix. 125–6).

> I start ! look ! hark ! but what in closed up sense
>   Was held, in open sense it flies away,
>   Leaving me naught but wailing eloquence.
> I, seeing better sights in sight's decay,
>   Called it anew, and wooed sleep again :
>   But him her host that unkind guest had slain.

Both Sidney and Milton found that one may see more clearly in a dream than when awake, and in both their dreams the lady *shines*.[1]

That the love-sonnet tradition lends its influence to Milton's lament is surely not without significance. For the tradition not only provides the poem's dramatic machinery, it also brings with it memories of the Petrarchan brand of lady-worship, —

> Love, sweetness, goodness, in her person shin'd

— artfully overlaid by Milton with biblical and classical attitudes. The result is a blend of the profoundest respect and tenderness.

In the first instance, however, a critic should ignore cross-fertilising traditions : instead he should relate each sonnet to its major conventions or topic, a sufficiently difficult task.

A topic much indulged in by Milton was the *praise* (IX, X, XIII, XV–XVII). Stereotyped already in classical times, such an address to a friend or notable public figure usually started with a compliment to a praiseworthy ancestor, if available, then listed either virtues or achievements, and encouraged virtues to persist or adjured the man of affairs to support a worthy cause. The style and compliment changed according to the subject's rank, god or potentate or private individual.[2] Milton, we may observe, seems to have thought it improper to found the fame of a man of public eminence upon any but his own achievements, and passes in silence over the ancestors of Fairfax, Cromwell and Vane,

---

[1] For some other similar parallels cf. Desportes, *Diane*, no. 35, R. Linche, *Diella* (1596), nos. 19, 24, Shakespeare, sonnet 43 ; and cf. below, p. 194.

[2] Aphthonius's well-known *Progymnasmata* dissected the *praise* and *execration* and other topics. Cf. also Quintilian's *Institutes* ii. 4. 20–21, iii. 7.

though the fathers of both Fairfax and Vane had served the Parliamentary side with distinction. Writing to the Lady (IX), whose identity was perhaps to be kept secret, he mentioned not blood-relations but spiritual ancestors, Mary and Ruth; Henry Lawes (XIII) was similarly placed, with the aid of a 'professional relative', Casella.

One type of praise very familiar in the seventeenth century has almost completely disappeared: complimentary verses to authors. Milton's lines on Shakespeare are of this kind, as is his sonnet to Lawes (XIII). Naturally the complimentary poet emphasised not only the author's general achievement but tried to help him to sell the work in hand, Shakespeare's *unvalu'd Book* or Lawes's *Airs* (l. 8).

Perhaps sonnet X (*Daughter to that good Earl*) was written for a similar purpose. Both Milton's avowedly commendatory verses, *On Shakespeare* and the sonnet to Lawes, failed to reach print immediately, the first having to wait two years till the publication of the Second Folio (1632), and the sonnet likewise remaining unprinted for two years (cf. p. 128). Milton wrote these tributes in good time, long before they were required. Is it not possible, then, that he was shown a biographical account of the Earl of Marlborough by the earl's daughter, perhaps intended as a preface to one of his legal works, and once again wrote complimentary verses prematurely? We know that Lady Margaret's father left a mass of unpublished manuscripts, some of which were being prepared for the press in the years to which we may assign the sonnet.[1]

If, as is usually agreed, Milton's sonnets were occasional poems,

---

[1] Cf. Ley's *Learned Treatise Concerning Wards and Liveries* (1641, 1642). His *Reports of Divers Resolutions* (1659) were probably held up by the civil wars, and other treatises from his pen lay ready (cf. the *Dictionary of National Biography*). As the sales of a law-book depended on the reputation of its author it was not uncommon at this time, in issuing a posthumous work, to include a biography or brief commendation listing his offices and praising his excellent decisions and personal virtues: cf. Coke's account of Littleton in the *Institutes*, etc.

we have to ask what occasion, if any, lies behind the sonnet to Lady Margaret Ley. According to Masson and other editors, Lady Margaret's conversation apparently 'ran much upon her father and his private and political virtues; and Milton listened respectfully . . .'.[1]   Certainly this is a possible interpretation. Yet an ordinary *praise* traditionally commenced with, but would not sustain to the end, an allusion to the praised one's parent or ancestor: the conceit with which Milton concludes, that a writer's description of a great man reflects the great man's qualities in himself, was on the contrary a commonplace in the *genre* of commendatory verses,[2] and the threefold emphasis upon Lady Margaret's descriptive powers points in the same direction.

The *execration* or *vituperation* could follow the pattern of the praise, pouring scorn on the subject's ancestors, listing his follies or vices, and so on. Decorum prescribed a colloquial style and permitted the name-calling which plays so prominent a part in sonnets XI, XII and *New Forcers*. In these three poems we come close to the classical epigram, from which the sonnet is sometimes said to originate: for example, XI and XII should be compared with Martial's epigrams to a detractor, to a reader difficult to please, etc.

Perhaps the most fascinatingly 'traditional' sonnet of all is XIX (*When I consider*). Its biblical allusions are well known: but the vast body of religious and meditative verse which transformed them into poetic clichés seems less familiar, for notes in the learned periodicals continue to call attention to stray Miltonic 'sources' and 'analogues' in English poetry — most of which could be multiplied a hundredfold by a diligent searcher. In

---

[1] Masson, *Life*, iii. 60.
[2] As in Robert Harvey's verses to Massinger, on *The Roman Actor*:
> Each line speaks him an emperor, every phrase
> Crowns thy deserving temples with the bays;
> So that reciprocally both agree,
> Thou liv'st in him, and he survives in thee.
>
> (*Massinger*, ed. Gifford (1813), I. clvi)

order to underline this purely traditional element in the sonnet I cite below some of the many 'parallels' in Henry Lok's religious sonnet-cycles (1597), never before mentioned, I believe, in this connection.

> (i) I Thee beseech, my purpose so to blesse,
>   That I a good *account* to Thee may make :
> (ii) I doe not hope my paines so deare to sell,
>   As they that beare the brunt and heate of day,
> (iii) Within Thy house this bodie base of mine,
>   It pleasèd Thee, O Lord ! my soule to plant,
>   A steward of *the gifts the which were Thine* . . .
> (iv) The *talent* which Thou pleasedst Lord to giue,
>   To me Thy seruant that I should bestow,
>   Whilst in *Thy seruice* on the Earth I liue,
>   My diligent increase thereof to show,
>   I haue abusèd Lord — too long — I know,
> (v) All creatures of the ayre, *the sea and land*,
>   Are players *at His appointment* of some thing,
> (vi) Yet with simplicitie of doue receaue
>   The *yoke* of law, whose rule they must fulfill,
>   And suffer *patiently* . . .[1]

In addition, Lok and Milton employed the same opening formula, a well-worn one : '*When I consider* of the holy band . . .'.[2] And — this may cause more surprise — Lok also made much of the blindness-motif :

> (vii) Borne *blinde* I was, through sinfull Adam's fall,
>   And neuer since could see with carnall eyes :
>   Ne know I where or how for helpe to call,
>   From out of sin to holie life to rise.[3]

The commonplace that post-lapsarian man is spiritually blind may be touched on in Milton's second line (*dark world and wide*: cf.

---

[1] Quoted from A. B. Grosart's edition, *Miscellanies of the Fuller Worthies' Library* (1871), ii. pp. 99, 107, 140, 153, 186, 204. Several of Lok's commonplaces occur more than once, e.g. man's gifts are God's gifts (iii) on pp. 244, 248, the talent (iv) on pp. 176, 248. In (ii) Lok refers to the parable of the vineyard, as does Milton in *day-labour*.

[2] P. 277. Cf. Shakespeare, sonnet 15 : '*When I consider* every thing that grows'.　　　　　　　　　　　　　[3] P. 118; cf. pp. 146, 152.

note). Otherwise this use of the blindness-theme only illustrates the fortuitous interlacings of the tradition.

By comparing the sonnets with traditional topics we often learn something about their meaning. Yet, if we are not careful, the tradition can also mislead. Sonnets XX and XXI (*Lawrence* and *Cyriack, whose Grandsire*) are usually described as 'Horatian invitations'.[1] Milton's topic admittedly goes back to Horace and other classical poets, yet his were not necessarily invitations of the same sort. He wrote to Lawrence as to a friend whom he sometimes met on walks, and literally asks 'where shall we meet now that walks are out of the question ?' The primary purpose is not to arrange a particular gaudy day but rather to suggest closer friendship, or at least to forestall the slackening of friendship. In short, where other poets interpolated professions of love as they outlined their hospitable intentions, Milton thought of friendship as the grand affair and left it to Lawrence to issue the first invitation, if he so desired. Walter Raleigh, who commented smilingly that in this sonnet the poet emerges as a 'poor boon companion',[2] totally misunderstood the delicacy of the situation.

As for XXI, it is a plausible conjecture that the invitation to *drench* deep thoughts *in mirth* called Skinner to a party; the allusion to *Wine* in XX perhaps confirms it. Yet if to a party, the invitation was sent indecently late ('*To day* deep thoughts resolve with me to drench'). I suspect that the sonnet is a *second* invitation to a young friend who had excused himself, an appeal for companionship much more pressing than that directed to Lawrence. Despite its superficial resemblances to Horace's bantering ode to Quintius Hirpinus (II. xi) this is a sonnet of barely disguised rebuke, far removed from the spirit of the Horatian invitation.

The ancestry of Milton's sonnets will now be sufficiently clear. But it should be added that a deliberate traditionalism is often

---

[1] Cf. pp. 74, 180.   [2] Raleigh, *Milton*, p. 8.

also at work in the realms of imagery, allusion and even of attitude. Not restrictively — the forward-looking Puritan of the mid-century certainly makes himself felt — but as an historical force by means of which the poet wishes us to judge his intellectual vitality. He asks us to consider the interpenetration of the biblical, classical, medieval, renaissance and puritan in his own mind, the cross-fertilising traditions that I have already mentioned. To appreciate this interpenetration it is, of course, necessary to pursue 'sources' — to separate *Tuskan Ayre* and the *Lillie and Rose, that neither sow'd nor spun* in sonnet XX (*Lawrence*) from their prevailingly 'classical' surroundings, and to observe that the success of this strange mixture depends partly upon the strong now-emphasis of the opening lines, the heavy frame that holds the rest together, and partly upon the identifiable personality of the poet (cf. p. 70).

And if traditionalism never chokes Milton's originality (except, perhaps, in XIV, where he not improperly subdues himself in an epitaph), it interferes no more with his sincerity. The genuineness of his praise was not compromised because he shaped it according to time-honoured conventions. He may laugh at Charles I for ascribing '*all vertue* to his Wife, in straines that come almost to Sonnetting',[1] but stops short of suggesting that such strains would be out of place in a sonnet. Should he himself fall back upon hackneyed compliments, as in presenting Vane as the 'ideal counsellor', he does so to make the point that Vane measures up to that ideal : as always, he wants the 'tradition' to be recognised.[2]

---

[1] *Eikonoklastes* (*C.M.* v. 139).

[2] In this section I have dealt with the impact of the tradition upon Milton's sonnets. For Milton's influence on later sonneteers the reader may be referred to R. D. Havens, *The Influence of Milton on English Poetry* (Harvard University Press, 1922, 1961).

III. TEXT

THREE collections of his minor poems contain between them all the sonnets of Milton now known: a manuscript in Trinity College, Cambridge, includes autograph versions of many, with sometimes more than one draft of the same poem, as well as scribal copies; the edition of the *Poems* dated 1645 printed sonnets I–X; and the edition of 1673 reprinted I–X, and added all that follow except XV, XVI, XVII and XXII (*Fairfax, Cromwell, Vane* and *Cyriack, this three years day*, which, commemorating the achievements of Parliamentarians, it would have been injudicious to publish after the Restoration). Milton seems to have given every care to the 1645 edition, and even when blind to have supervised the writing down of his poetry quite exactingly, so that, as most of the editors agree, his final intention scarcely ever remains in doubt.[1]

Several of the sonnets appeared first in print in books other than Milton's own: that to Lawes in the composer's *Choice Psalms*, 1648, that to Vane in G. Sikes's *The Life and Death of Sir Henry Vane*, 1662, and the four omitted from the edition of 1673 at the end of Edward Phillips's Preface in his edition of Milton's *Letters of State*, 1694. The first two (Lawes and Vane) exhibit no important variants compared with other authorised versions, and need not detain us; of Phillips's text of the four sonnets, on the other hand, something more must be said.

[1] There is some doubt about his spellings: cf. p. 56. Hereafter I sometimes refer to the three primary texts as MS. (or, Cambridge MS.), 1645 and 1673. All three are reproduced in facsimile in Harris Fletcher's *John Milton's Complete Poetical Works*, vol. i (Urbana, 1943), though the best facsimile of the MS. remains W. A. Wright's (Cambridge, 1899). For some of the blunders of the 1673 edition cf. Hanford, *Handbook*, pp. 393–5.

All the editors seem to have assumed that Phillips's text was corrupt.[1] Obvious perversions, of a sort made familiar by the memorially contaminated texts of Shakespeare, amply support their view :

> CRomwell our Chief of Men, that through a Croud,
> Not of War only, but distractions rude . . .

Nevertheless two variants in the sonnet to Vane raise another possibility. The first and thirteenth lines stand in Phillips as

> VANE, Young in years, but in Sage Councels old,
> Therefore on thy Right hand Religion leans,

and tally with deleted readings in the Cambridge MS. :

> Vane, young in yeares but in sage counsell [*orig.* counsells] old,
> Therfore on thy firme [*orig.* right] hand religion leanes

We cannot escape the deduction that Phillips in these two lines recalled a draft of the sonnet earlier than that inserted in the Cambridge MS. And as either Edward or his brother John Phillips was the 'Kinsman that was then with him' in June 1652, when the sonnet was composed,[2] it would be the most natural thing in the world for Edward to have acted as his uncle's scribe for an early draft, or to have seen and memorised one taken down by John. Aubrey knew, in fact, that Phillips possessed versions of some sonnets omitted from the 1673 edition — 'but he hath hung back these 2 yeares, as to imparting copies to me'.[3] That was in 1684, and therefore Phillips's texts are not necessarily as bad as one would suppose from a lapse of twenty years (i.e

[1] Cf. Smart, p. 120; Darbishire, *Poetical Works*, ii. 324. Miss Darbishire in her collation quotes the 1694 text of *Vane*, l. 13, as 'firme', an error which would encourage the 'corrupt text' theory (ii. 326).

[2] Cf. p. 157, below, and Masson, *Life*, iv. 431.

[3] Quoted *Lives*, p. 342. Phillips probably could not consult the MS. in 1694, for this seems to have passed into the keeping of Trinity College with other 'old papers' once the property of Sir Henry Newton Puckering. Puckering's books went to the College in 1691 : though Milton's MS. was not named in the catalogue, we must assume that it was no longer in the hands of his family. Cf. W. A. Wright's *Facsimile*, p. 1.

Milton's death to 1694): corrupt though they are, *some* of his variants may derive from his recollection of the sonnets in their earliest states. As it is not always possible to distinguish authorial variants from memorial errors I therefore cite all Phillips's variants in my Collation, though conscious that corruption will have come more easily to Phillips than second thoughts to Milton.

The 'old spelling' of my edition requires some explanation. An editor can choose between two types of copy-text (the Cambridge Manuscript, or the printed versions of 1645 and 1673), or he may prepare an old-spelling 'reformed text'. Jotting down his poems in the manuscript Milton did not always take care to be consistent, and therefore one hesitates to adopt his autograph spellings; on the other hand, his printed texts, though no doubt based on copy representing the author's final intention, were less meticulously produced than has been widely assumed, some of the spellings deriving not from Milton but from scribes or compositors.[1]   A reformed text, again, raises the difficulty that the poet's spelling habits changed over the years — should one, then, revert to the presumed spelling at the time of composition, or to that at the time of the author's final revision (1673) ?   I have decided to follow the printed texts, on the hypothesis that Milton regarded most of those scribal-compositorial spellings that he tolerated as indifferent: he checked the spelling of distinctive words to which he attached importance, and the occasional respelling of some of the remaining words did not trouble him. We, too, may therefore content ourselves with the printed versions, even though they dropped a few Miltonic spellings (e.g. thir=their).

A minor change against which Milton struggled for years will

---

[1] For reformed texts cf. Darbishire, *Poetical Works*, and B. A. Wright, *Milton's Poems* (Everyman's Library, 1956); for scribal and compositorial spellings, articles by J. T. Shawcross in *H.L.Q.* (1962–3), xxvi. 351–61, and *P.M.L.A.* (1963), lxxviii. 501–10.

show that an edition based on the printed texts of 1645 and 1673, despite all that can be said against it, enjoys real advantages. In the Cambridge Manuscript the first four autograph versions of sonnets (VII, IX, X and the first draft of XIII dated 9 February 1645/6) have no capitals at the beginning of the verse line, apart from the first lines of quatrains and tercets. Thereafter Milton tried to switch to capitals at the start of each line, a practice from which he lapsed in every autograph and, more noticeably, in every rough draft up to and including the last sonnet written in his own hand (XV). In the 1645 edition Milton's new method of starting every line with a capital was already employed, so we may take it that in the two drafts of XIII and XIV and in the single drafts of XI, XII and XV he invariably failed to carry through his policy. To follow the manuscript would result in chaos, while the reformed text based on Milton's contemporary habits would have to accept his original policy for sonnets I–X, and perhaps for XIII. Here, as with some other textual difficulties, a reformed text based on the author's final intention would of course agree with the edition of 1673.

My copy-text is, therefore, the first printed version of each sonnet — excepting XV, XVI, XVII and XXII, for which the Cambridge Manuscript serves as copy.[1] I emend only obvious misprints, and record in the Collation all variants in the early texts — but not all variations in spelling and punctuation. With the Italian sonnets I have, like other editors, silently changed some of the punctuation and introduced accents and apostrophes not found in the originals.

By banishing all sonnet-titles from my text (all those attributable to Milton himself appear in the Collation) I have gone beyond 'the author's final intention' but, I think, have taken it to its

---

[1] In these four poems I depart from copy, however, to italicise proper names, in order to bring them into line with the other sonnets, where italics are almost always used for this purpose; and, for the same reason, print a capital at the start of XV. 8, and expand contractions.

logical conclusion. In the edition of 1673 Milton retained only three titles, which would help contemporaries to place public events of long ago. For the twentieth-century reader these events have ceased to be common knowledge (e.g. Henry Lawes no longer stirs the memory more powerfully than Lady Margaret Ley), so there is no point in allowing them to distract attention from the sonnets' serial development.[1]

For the identity of the scribes of those sonnets not entered in the Cambridge Manuscript by Milton himself the reader may consult M. Kelley, 'Milton's Later Sonnets', and J. T. Shawcross, 'Notes on Milton's Amanuenses' (*J.E.G.P.* (1959), lviii. 29–38).

---

[1] This is explained in the next section. Cf. p. 72 for the sonnet-titles in the 1673 edition.

IV. THE ORDER OF THE SONNETS

In the 1645 edition Milton numbered his sonnets I to X. The edition of 1673 continued this numbering, omitting four sonnets (cf. p. 54), its last one being thus headed XIX instead of XXIII. Other special features in 1673 were the switching round of XI and XII, and the exclusion of *New Forcers* from the sonnet sequence (it was placed eight pages after XIX, on p. 69). Milton, and later his scribes, also numbered the sonnets in the Cambridge Manuscript from XI onwards: here he first labelled XI and XII as in the present edition, and a scribe copied both and attached the same numbers, subsequently changing '11' to '12'. An afterthought also prompted the marginal note below XII — 'on yᵉ forcers of Conscience to come in heer'. In 1673, therefore, Milton retained one earlier change (XI and XII) but rejected the other (*New Forcers*).

No trace appears in the Cambridge Manuscript of three sonnets and four lines of a fourth, XVIII–XXI. 4: since XXI. 5–14 is succeeded by XXII and XXIII it has been plausibly conjectured that two leaves of the manuscript are missing.[1]

Despite the incompleteness of each one of Milton's three collections we are able to deduce from them the original numbering of all his sonnets. And this has naturally led to speculation about the order of their writing.

In the Cambridge Manuscript the transcript of the sonnet numbered 13 (p. 43) bears the date 'Feb. 9. 1645' (i.e. 1646). The manuscript title of the sonnet numbered 14 (p. [44]) reads '16 Decem. 1646.' The manuscript title of the sonnet numbered 15 (p. 47) refers to the

---

[1] Cf. Hanford, 'Milton's Sonnets', p. 477.

siege of Colchester, which took place in 1648. The manuscript title of the sonnet numbered 16 (p. 47) reads 'May 1652.' The sonnet numbered 17 (p. [48]) was delivered to Vane on July 3, 1652. And in the sonnet numbered 22 (p. 49), 'this three years day' indicates 1655, three years after Milton became blind in 1652. This consistent correspondence of larger number to later date clearly shows that in the Cambridge Manuscript Milton's numbers indicate the order in which he composed his later sonnets.

Maurice Kelley [1] expresses bluntly a view shared by many Milton scholars — that the arrangement of the sonnets in the Cambridge Manuscript and the two printed texts quite simply followed the order of composition. Nevertheless there are those who, while perhaps assenting in general terms, in the case of isolated sonnets disown the 'chronological principle', and they include some distinguished names. For example, J. H. Hanford has insisted that 'Stevens is in agreement with Masson and is undoubtedly right in dating sonnet XII (11) before sonnet XI (12)',[2] i.e. he abandons the sequence of the 1673 edition. Again, J. S. Smart, E. M. W. Tillyard, M. Y. Hughes, J. M. French and others refuse to date XIX (*When I consider*) as late as 1655, its *terminus a quo* if it follows XVIII (*Avenge O Lord*, where Milton describes the atrocities of April 1655). Exceptions so strongly supported invite some reconsideration of the 'principle'.[3]

It must be admitted that roughly half of Milton's English sonnets either date themselves or are dated in the Cambridge Manuscript, and seem to bear out a chronological arrangement. But what of the rest ? Before we jump to conclusions it will be well to hear Hanford, for the other side.

Hanford showed that XI and XII were very probably interchanged for publication, and, in addition, that there are reasons for doubting that these two sonnets were written consecutively.

---

[1] 'Milton's Later Sonnets', p. 20.   [2] Op. cit., p. 475.
[3] Others have challenged it in passing, e.g. W. R. Parker, *P.M.L.A.* (1958), lxxiii. 199–200 n.

For XI was entered in the manuscript after two drafts of XIII, while XII followed after two of XIV : even if Milton copied XI into the manuscript from elsewhere (its text is comparatively clean), enough deletions disfigure XII to make it certainly an early draft, and probably the very first. Hanford also compared the arrangement of the sonnets with that of the remaining poems of the 1645 edition, and submitted that in the edition Milton did not hesitate

to modify the chronological order of the other poems when there was good reason to do so. Thus he naturally preferred to begin the volume with the great 'Nativity Ode' (1629) rather than with the juvenile paraphrases of the Psalms. And in arranging the Latin elegies he placed Elegy VII at the end of the series though it had been written earlier than Elegy VI. None the less . . . [Milton] desired, other considerations being indifferent, to have the arrangement indicate a progression corresponding to his years (p. 482).

Masson expressed a similar view of the editions of 1645 and 1673 : 'on the whole, though in neither edition is the chronological principle of arrangement paramount, one can see that a subordinate respect was paid to it'.[1]

Another attack on the 'chronological principle' has been made by Fitzroy Pyle and C. J. Morse. They say that it

can be disproved by a simple *reductio ad absurdum*. XVIII (on the Piedmont massacre) cannot be before April, 1655 : XXII (on the third anniversary of his total blindness) cannot be later than September, 1655; yet between them comes XX (to Lawrence), a sonnet written in winter.[2]

In the arrangement of Milton's sonnets a 'chronological principle' certainly played its part. Kelley would make it 'paramount', at least in the later sonnets. I cannot agree : to establish

---

[1] *Poetical Works*, i. 114.

[2] Morse, *T.L.S.* (15 September 1961), p. 620; cf. Pyle, *R.E.S.* (1958), ix. 385 n. Merritt Y. Hughes (p. 168) thought this 'conclusive proof that the order of the sonnets in 1673 is not chronological'. I think it is a strong argument — but not coercive, since XXII need not refer to an anniversary (cf. p. 186), and XX may precede the winter (cf. p. 87 n.).

a general chronological progression is not to prove that Milton felt totally committed to this principle — any more than in the elegies, where one out of seven departs from the order of composition.[1]

What other principle could have interfered ? With a tradition-conscious poet like Milton we look instinctively into the past, as he must have done, when such a question is put — and help immediately arrives. For, though many classical texts were not published, and therefore not arranged, by their authors, various precedents would occur to Milton and deserve our pondering. First and foremost, the case of Horace.

That Horace himself published and arranged the sequence of his *Odes* no one nowadays disputes, except as regards detail. What method of arrangement did he adopt ? Here, of course, dispute becomes inevitable — though the various theories meet on a good deal of common ground.

We may at least gather that Horace contemplated a collection of poems being read continuously in such a way that the effect of a particular poem could be heightened or weakened by the sequence in which it was placed. . . .[2]

Faced with the problem of arrangement . . . [Horace] seized on any stray principle that suggested itself. . . . Here and there odes are put next to one another for some common factor; thus 1, 14 and 15 appear to be political allegories, 1, 27 and 28 are dramatic monologues, 1, 34 and 35 are both about Fortuna.[3]

---

[1] Kelley supported the case for 'chronological order' by urging 'that Milton's amanuenses regularly entered his later sonnets [in the Cambridge Manuscript] at the time when, or soon after, he had composed them' (op. cit., p. 23). He cited four examples (XVI, XVII, XIX and XXIII) which, even if sound, scarcely establish a regular practice. Milton need not have hurried to inscribe every new sonnet in the Cambridge Manuscript, since he evidently kept other copies of his poems. And we must remember that the manuscript really consists of 'two separate collections of Milton's verse, which were bound together in the eighteenth century' (Kelley, p. 21): if there was a 'regular practice', it would not necessarily be observed in both.

[2] *Quinti Horatii Flacci Opera Omnia*, ed. E. C. Wickham (Oxford, 1874–91, 2 vols.), i. 9.

[3] L. P. Wilkinson, *Horace and his Lyric Poetry* (Cambridge, 1946), p. 15.

At the other extreme W. Ludwig expounded a structural chiasmus in the first twelve odes of Book II which, even if not entirely convincing, at least recalls to mind the literary environment in which Horace worked.   It recalls Virgil's meticulous symmetry in the *Eclogues*, addressing his patron by name at i. 2, ii. 41, iii. 41, iv. 2 and similar mosaic-work.[1]   And it encouraged N. E. Collinge to develop an important critical perception both imaginatively and cautiously.

The texture of this body of lyric is made up, then, of manifold oppositions of whole poems.   There is one between the significant (artistically speaking) and the much more frequent insignificant juxtaposing of odes, for it is folly to think that even most of the odes are grouped according to some master-plan;   there is another between the continuation of a mood and its dissipation;   yet another between the continuation of a mood or atmosphere and the continuation of topic or factual references or setting. . . .[2]

The sense of continuity, Mr Collinge shows, sometimes depends on the sustaining of a general subject in a 'block' of odes, sometimes on inobtrusive devices, verbal repetitions ('rivets') such as *mecum* in ii. 6.1 and ii. 7.1, or contrasts

like the antithesis of the unsuccessful and successful escape from hell at the close of, respectively, ii. 18 and 19. . . . What really happens, if Horace speaks of the same thing, more or less, in a close sequence of odes, is that the reader's mind is held in a certain receptive poise rather than in a fixed logical groove (p. 41).

The 'iterative imagery' traced by modern critics in Shakespeare's plays has much the same function as the 'rivets' in Horace ; and Shakespeare's sonnets also establish a relationship to each other in the realms of imagery and allusion independently of the logic of story or argument.   For example, the first sonnet, in which the poet urges the noble youth to marry and to leave the world an heir, ends with the couplet,

[1] Cf. N. E. Collinge, *The Structure of Horace's Odes* (1961), p. 37, and also J. R. Watson in *Essays in Criticism* (1964), xiv. 148–55, for the symmetry in *P.L.*
[2] *Ibid.*, pp. 52–3.

> Pitty the world, or else this glutton be,
> To eate the worlds due, by the graue and thee.

The second begins :

> When fortie Winters shall beseige thy brow,
> And digge deep trenches in thy beauties field,

— and, Shakespeare goes on, if the youth were asked 'where all thy beautie lies',

> To say within thine owne deepe sunken eyes,
> Were an all-eating shame, and thriftlesse praise.

Who can doubt that the *graue* suggested the *deep trenches* and then *deepe sunken eyes*, or that *an all-eating shame* refers back to *eate the worlds due* ?

In many seventeenth-century poetical collections the verbal and atmospheric continuity generally conceded in Shakespeare's sonnets is to be found divorced from all pretence of a story. Crashaw placed in sequence *The Weeper, The Tear* and his epigram on 'the water of our Lord's Baptism', for sufficiently obvious reasons (*Steps to the Temple*, 1646). But the poets who, at this time, excelled in the art of implication could also set to work more discreetly.

> This verse marks that, and both do make a motion
> Unto a third, that ten leaves off doth lie

wrote George Herbert. And, although he referred to the verses of the Bible, he might have described some seventeenth-century writers, such as Donne or Vaughan,[1] in the same words. The juxtaposing of superficially unrelated poems was not always innocent — and this has a bearing on the sonnets of Milton, in which a sense of continuity might also be developed without the aid of the story machinery of older sonnet-cycles.

---

[1] Cf. E. C. Pettet, 'The Unity and Continuity of *Silex Scintillans*' in *Of Paradise and Light* (Cambridge, 1960).

A deliberate collocation of some of Milton's sonnets according to subject or implicit ideas cannot be denied : IX and X (*Lady* and *Daughter to that good Earl*), XI and XII (*I did but prompt the age* and *A Book was writ of late*), XV–XVII (*Fairfax, Cromwell* and *Vane*), XXI and XXII (*Cyriack, whose Grandsire* and *Cyriack, this three years day*) go together in so far as they address virtuous ladies, protest against the same detraction, celebrate three great public figures, and address the same friend. But XXI (*Cyriack, whose Grandsire*) also connects with XX (*Lawrence*), both being 'invitations',[1] and this suggests that just as there are groups of poems there are also threads between groups.

Milton's intentions in placing side by side sonnets related in theme or atmosphere emerge distinctly when we turn to the one whose date has been most fiercely disputed — *When I consider* (XIX). Whether or not this poem followed immediately after *Avenge O Lord* (XVIII) in the sequence of writing, excellent reasons dictated its present position. Both XVIII and XIX celebrate God's terrible way with His chosen, the slaughtered saints and the talented poet deprived of his sight. And not only is there an important kinship of subject : we should grow conscious also of other resemblances. There is a similar sense of spaciousness in the sonnets. And at the same point in each (l. 12) Milton discusses the *triple Tyrant* and the *kingly* state of God, and at the same point again (l. 14) hopes that generations unborn *may fly* the one, and proposes to *stand and waite* to serve the other. The *yoak* imposed by Milton's God appears all the more *milde* if 'the reader's mind is held in a certain receptive poise' from sonnet XVIII to XIX, and the poet's *murmur* sounds the more ungrateful if one still hears the *moans* of the unfortunate mountaineers. Reading XIX after XVIII one finds a new dimension in the self-criticism of the more personal poem.

When I consider, in addition, creates a new field of force within

[1] But cf. p. 52.

which the two next sonnets, the 'invitations' to Lawrence and Skinner (XX and XXI), lose some of their autonomy. In XIX Milton at first regrets the uselessness of his talent, then decides to submit to circumstances and God's will: the invitations advise a similar submission to circumstances, the *hard Season* or the *cheerful hour* sent by God, and with it some relaxation from the pursuit of one's talent. We might say that Milton passes on the lesson he had himself learnt (indeed, the invitations may illustrate what is implied at the end of XIX by *stand and waite*).[1] As in the transition from XVIII to XIX there is some shift of tone, but not therefore a complete severance of subject or of implication.

Why, it may now be asked, does XXII (*Cyriack, this three years day*) not accompany XIX (*When I consider*), irrefutably related as the two sonnets are in dealing with the poet's blindness? In reply we have only to observe that a third sonnet (XXIII) also turns on the same subject and joins on to XXII more satisfactorily. The affirmation that the blind poet never enjoys the sight of sun, or moon, or star, or man *or woman* (XXII) surely holds our minds 'in a certain receptive poise' for the opening of XXIII, 'Methought I *saw my late espoused Saint . . .*' More than that, the switch from the public image of the poet as he desired it (in XXII), *content*, *bearing up*, strong in *heart* and *hope*, to the spectacle of his private anguish in XXIII, gives depth to both poems: we see XXII more clearly as an exercise in 'cheering oneself up', and the poignancy of Milton's grief for his wife gains in effect coming as it does just after his solemn declaration (in XXII) that he has no regrets. In passing we may also notice that Milton emphasises in XXII. 2 and XXIII. 5 the surprising absence of *blemish* and *spot*, and of *spot* and *taint*, a perhaps quite unconscious association.

To clarify the continuity in Milton's arrangement of the sonnets I propose, next, to comment upon a few of the many examples

---

[1] Cf. Fitzroy Pyle in *R.E.S.* (1958), ix. 384.

of contact. That the Italian sonnets (II–VI) and Canzone form a self-contained unit is, of course, manifest. And the function of the first English sonnet, as an introduction to the Italian poems, has already struck several commentators — though not, perhaps, all the details governed by it. The nightingale, the mate of both the Muse and Love (I. 13), melts into the Italian lady who sings so sweetly and compels the poet's love. The imagery of I and II reinforces the symbol : the nightingale's *bloomy Spray* leads into *l' herbosa val* (the flowery vale) and *Là, onde l' alta tua virtù s' infiora* (there, where *blooms* thy lofty might) ; the bird's *soft lay* prepares for the lady's *spirto gentil* (gentle spirit), and the *amorous power* of its song for the *disio amoroso* (amorous longing) induced by the lady.

I shall say no more about the Italian poems, except that the last one (VI) links quite naturally with the second English sonnet (VII). Addressing the Italian lady, Milton describes himself as 'covetous of genius and lofty worth, and of the sounding lyre and of the Muses' — and VII then dilates upon his hopes as a poet. In each poem rueful reflections about Milton's innocently youthful appearance introduce these high-aspiring hopes. The idea of flying away from oneself also appears in both :

> Giovane piano, e semplicetto amante,
>> Poi che fuggir me stesso in dubbio sono,

[Young, gentle and simple lover that I am, and in doubt how to fly from myself. . . .]

> How soon hath Time, the suttle theef of youth,
>> Stoln on his wing my three and twentith yeer !
>> My hasting dayes flie on with full career, . . .

and in both Milton makes a fervent dedication, of his heart to his lady, of himself to his talent and his Maker.

There are similar threads between some sonnets that, at first glance, appear to be utterly disconnected, such as XII and XIII (*A Book was writ of late* and the sonnet to Lawes). For these two

poems the art of composition, both literary and musical, nevertheless serves as a common subject. (*Tertrachord*, being a musical
term, also brings them together.) Milton's *Tertrachordon* was
wov'n close, both matter, form and stile : Quintilian is dragged in
to illustrate the standards aimed at ; Lawes took the same care
to write *well measur'd Song* and *to span Words with just note and
accent*, that is, to correlate the elements of his art. In particular
Milton deplores any forcing of the language whereby rugged
outlandish names *to our like mouths grow sleek* (XII), and then
congratulates Lawes on not forcing the language, for the composer
with smooth air could *humor best our tongue* (XIII). There is also
a similarity when Milton stands aloof from the *file* of stall-readers
and Lawes is exempted *from the throng*, and another when XII
concludes with the picture of King Edward being taught by
Cheke and XIII with that of Dante listening to Casella. Moreover, the allusion to Cheke, who *taught* his *age* and created a new
generation of Greek scholars in England, coming at the end of
XII, parallels the compliment at the opening of XIII that Lawes
first *taught* the new style of English music, for which he will be
honoured in *after-age*.

The word *taught* mortises these two sonnets together. Dante's
Casella, at the end of XIII, leads into the beginning of XIV in the
same way, though perhaps not so patently. Casella, we have to
remember, arrived in Purgatory conducted by the Angel of
Faith — and the Faith that ripened Mrs Thomason's soul to dwell
with God (XIV. 1) is, of course, imagined as an angel. The
mention of *Purgatory* (XIII. 14) perhaps also led to the idea that
a just soul must be *ripen'd . . . to dwell with God* (XIV),[1] even
though Milton thought in Protestant, not Roman Catholic,
terms. Both sonnets, again, play with the idea of 'lending wings':
Verse must lend her wing To honour thee, and *Faith . . . clad them*

[1] For example, cf. Dante's *Purgatory*, xix. 91 : 'Spirit, in whom weeping ripens
(*matura*) that without which man cannot turn to God.'

o're with purple beams And azure wings. Finally, Milton commends both Lawes and Mrs Thomason by means of pairs of related abstractions, *song* and *verse*, *faith* and *love*, which almost displace the person addressed in the foreground of each sonnet; and both Lawes and Mrs Thomason are said to have served their respective abstractions, and are then rewarded by them.

Some of the larger thematic links between sonnets can now be mentioned quite briefly. Sonnet VIII follows on from VII in presenting a poet more assured of his powers but still very much preoccupied with this subject. In both VIII and IX the poet applauds *pity and ruth* and deprecates *anger*: and no doubt *deed of honour* and *gentle acts* (VIII. 3, 6) are to be compared with the virtuous young lady's more admirable *deeds of light* (IX. 10). Liberty, the cardinal theme in XI, makes a preliminary appearance in X, and in both poems love of liberty implies love of goodness. Sonnets XIV and XV immortalise *firm unshak'n vertue*, in a woman meekly living a private life, and in a soldier very much in the public eye. Fairfax's *name in armes through Europe rings*: Mrs Thomason's good works *spake the truth of thee in glorious Theams / Before the Judge*. The generosity of the one is rewarded with *azure wings*, the other has to combat *serpent wings*, *Fraud*, *Avarice* and *Rapine* — a contrast, surely, of two kinds of Christian warrior.

Just as sonnets XV to XVIII deal more and more overtly with religious intolerance, sonnets XIX to XXIII form a group as personal revelations — like sonnets I to VII, another 'personal' group. A special relationship may even have been intended for the first sonnet and the last. Each of the two is a 'night-piece', in each the poet longs for an unattainable love, and in each a sudden interruption (from the cuckoo's song, from daybreak) can rob him of his love and reminds him of *my hopeles doom* and *my night*: strange coincidences, giving a circular effect which makes us conscious both of the poet's more or less fixed personality and of the repetitions in his experiences, and therefore reinforces the sense of continuity in the sonnets as a whole.[1] In Milton's Latin *Elegies* there is a similar arrangement, the first and the last disclosing his susceptibility to girlish charm, a subject dropped in the intervening poems.   The parallel is even more extraordinary : in Elegy I, as in the first sonnet (*O Nightingale*) the poet's excited anticipation of love has no particular object ; in the last elegy he describes how, having glimpsed an unknown girl in a London crowd, he was overcome by love — but, 'while I suffered, she who alone could give me happiness was carried away, never to return to my eyes again' : just so his last sonnet records that he caught sight of his *late espoused Saint* in a dream, and that she also disappeared for ever.

It should now be plain that the prevalent opinion about the arrangement of the sonnets is not satisfactory. 'When passing from one to the other there is no continuity, as in a sequence ; the tone and point of view instantly change.'[2] We must agree that the idea of a Petrarchan sequence never entered Milton's mind : none the less this should not rule out the possibility of another kind of continuity, one perhaps not incapable of accommodating instant changes of tone and point of view. The various verbal, tonal and allusive 'rivets' outlined above serve this impressionistic continuity, to which Milton was no doubt drawn by both classical and English poets, Virgil, Horace, Shakespeare, Donne, Herbert and many more.

Milton's self-concentration also adds, and quite decisively, to the sense of coherence in the sonnets. One thinks in the first place of *How soon hath Time* and *When I consider* and *Cyriack, this three years day* (VII, XIX and XXII), yet the Miltonic ethos is elaborated directly or indirectly in every sonnet, and the sonnets

---

[1] Todd recognised a similarity on these two sonnets : 'Milton's first and last Sonnets display . . . the sweetness and tenderness of Petrarch' (vi. 438). Masson called XIX–XXII 'four private Sonnets', and thought that 'the four will be read best in connexion' (*Life*, v. 236–7).   [2] Smart, p. 43 ; cf. Pattison, p. 51.

as a series reflect his personality more vividly than any other single work — comparing in this, on a slightly reduced scale, with Horace's *Odes*. Praising or dispraising, Milton usually makes us conscious of two ways of life, one of them his own : sometimes he explicitly identifies himself with a party ('Cromwell, *our* cheif of men . . . Helpe *us*'), but even when he does not, as in writing of Fairfax, he implicitly ranges himself behind *firm unshak'n vertue* against *Violence* and *Fraud*. Indeed, Milton seems obsessed by the struggles of virtue towards self-fulfilment — witness the frequent emphasis on the need to surrender to the will of Heaven, and the comparison of brutal war and *gentle acts* (VIII), of *the Hill of heav'nly Truth* and *the broad way and the green* (IX), of noble virtues and corruption (X), of the *bloody Piemontese* and the *slaughter'd Saints* (XVIII), of impatient and patient attitudes to God (XIX), and so on. At times this major preoccupation of the sonnets was narrowed to deal with a specific evil, intolerance (XI, XII, XV–XVIII and *New Forcers*). And another favourite Miltonic subject, 'good art and the good artist', found expression in I, VII, XI–XIII, XX and XXII, in some cases combined with the virtue-vice antithesis : the nightingale, for example, is the 'bird of love' and opposes *the rude Bird of Hate* not only as a symbol but by exposing *the shallow Cuccoo's bill* with its own *liquid notes*, or superior art.

In short, we are made to feel that the poet cannot escape certain all-important ideas, because he identifies himself with them so completely. And, of course, Milton's very style reinforces this impression of his self-concentration and of his personal and continuous presence, just as it does in *Paradise Lost*, where it acted similarly as a unifying device. Moreover, the early sonnets are personally so revealing — the one to the virtuous young lady (IX) being, for example, indirectly self-descriptive — that we have no difficulty thereafter in identifying the style and the man.

A significant departure in the printed texts from the Cambridge

M.S.—F

Manuscript emphasises the personality of the poet in another way. With three understandable exceptions, Milton suppressed the titles of all his sonnets : [1] they stand under the general heading 'Sonnets', and are numbered. The omission of the titles plays down the occasional nature of the poems which, if dwelt upon, could easily deflect attention from their continuity ; on the other hand, the numbers strengthen the impression of continuity. Read through as a numbered series the sonnets chronicle one man's reactions to the events and individuals of his time, one man's self-exploration and exploration of values, he, the poet, remaining the common factor and a rival centre of interest even when the ostensible subject is a nightingale or Oliver Cromwell.

To sum up, then, the reasons against the theory of chronological arrangement. (i) While it is true that many of the sonnets observe chronological order, Milton's *Elegies* and *Poems* of 1645 and 1673 do so too as a rule, though not without exception : in the sonnets, therefore, similar exceptions should cause no surprise. (ii) Such exceptions can be explained by means of another principle, which imposes on the sonnets a form of continuity also found in Milton's most admired predecessors in the art of poetry, Horace, Shakespeare, etc. (iii) Many of Milton's most distinguished editors and critics disallow the chronological principle in one instance or another, and consequently discredit it in general. (iv) Milton himself switched the numbering of two sonnets (XI and XII), and entered sonnets in the Cambridge Manuscript out of numerical order — strong presumptive evi-

[1] In the 1673 edition Milton linked XI to XII (numbered the other way round) with the title '*On the same*', headed XIII '*To Mr. H. Lawes, on his Aires*', and XVIII '*On the late Massacher in* Piemont'. Lawes was named because, addressed simply as 'Harry', he is represented as a person who ought to be publicly identifiable — and XVIII perhaps retained its title in 1673 because, though concerned with an overseas event of eighteen years before, this still lingered in the public mind.

dence that he was willing to disregard chronology in his final arrangement.

Since months, and even years, separate some neighbouring sonnets that can be accurately dated, even unconscious 'rivets' and contacts indicate that Milton thought of these poems as related, and that he referred back to what was previously written as he added to them. In view of the time-gap, unconscious echoes in adjacent sonnets confirm that *something goes before*. (Most of the echoes are, I think, quite conscious, and establish continuity more straightforwardly.) It seems, therefore, that a serial principle conflicts with the chronological principle of arrangement — or rather, that it may do so in some few instances. For, after all, there is no reason to doubt that, generally speaking, the sonnet series followed the line of least resistance, the line of time.

In suggesting a serial interest in the sonnets I do not, of course, deny that they are occasional poems : for the serial and occasional requirements did not have to conflict, though their relative importance shifts from case to case. A comparison with *In Memoriam* can here be of help. We know that Tennyson finished first the parts now numbered IX, XXX, XXXI, LXXXV and XXVIII, and that, though supporting the structure of the work with a pronounced internal chronology, he 'did not choose to make the internal chronology coincide with the actual order of events'.[1] Many of Tennyson's poems are occasional, yet they fit into the series — and some were fitted in at the wrong place, historically speaking. If Tennyson, professedly writing a personal story, switched round some of his individual poems, Milton might well retain a loose chronological framework and similarly insert some poems out of place.

---

[1] Cf. A. C. Bradley, *A Commentary on Tennyson's in Memoriam*, 1901, pp. 14, 21 n. Bradley's authority for the list of sections first written, the poet's son, slightly changed the list, but this does not affect my argument.

How does the new theory affect interpretation ? Most start-
lingly in recognising continuity, and thus at once denying the
discrete existence of the various sonnets and raising the twenty-
three sonnets together to the dignity of a single, considered work
of art. Not that one should claim 'organic unity' of the more
rigorous sort, 'wov'n close, both matter, form and stile'; rather,
one finds a looser unity, which — leaving aside Horace and
Shakespeare — suited the genius of many great artists, the Bacon
of the *Essays*, Browne in *Religio Medici* and Donne in the *Songs
and Sonets*: a unity centring, in the last resort, on the writer's
definitive personality, and not wholly unrelated to a tradition of
discursive literature as hospitable to Italian Epic as to *Tristram
Shandy*.

Interpretation is also affected in that sonnets previously dated
by their place in the 'order' can no longer be so conveniently
disposed of — e.g. I–VI, VIII–XII, XIX–XXI and XXIII. And
as soon as we doubt the general order we must feel uneasy about
the precise occasion of some of these sonnets : accordingly, it
becomes unnecessary to suppose, with Masson, that the sonnets
to Lawrence and Skinner (XX and XXI) 'are cards of invitation
to little parties, *perhaps to one and the same little party*, in Milton's
house'.[1] In discussing these sonnets of uncertain date I try to
suggest alternative possibilities, which, if it serves no other purpose, will at least dissipate false confidence about their occasion
and, at times, about their meaning.

As has been mentioned, the arrangement of the sonnets in the
1673 edition differed in three respects from Milton's original
intentions : (i) he changed round XI and XII, (ii) he excluded
New Forcers from the sonnet sequence, (iii) he omitted XV, XVI,
XVII and XXII. It seems reasonable to assume, with other

[1] Masson, *Life*, v. 239; my italics. But was XX an invitation to Milton's
house ? Cf. p. 52.

editors, that (iii) resulted from the altered political situation after
the Restoration. Very likely (i) was also a late afterthought, a
concomitant, perhaps, of the decision to drop the sonnet-titles
(cf. p. 72) — for there was no great need for the allusion to
'certain treatises', in his common title for XI and XII, if *Tetrachordon* was named in XII before the reader comes to XI.

As regards (ii), Milton seems to have changed his mind three
or four times about *New Forcers*. A copy of the poem now lost
seems to have stood in the Cambridge Manuscript at one time;
an autograph note after XII (cf. p. 59) indicates that this position
probably replaces another. Being autograph, the note dates from
before 1652. A scribal copy with corrections also follows XVII
(*Vane*), and must therefore be dated after July 1652; and the
edition of 1673 removed the sonnet once more.

Clearly Milton could not make up his mind about *New Forcers*:
his several changes suggest real uncertainty, and I therefore accept
his final decision. In the case of XI, XII, XV–XVII and XXII,
however, expediency compelled his changes, and so I revert to
his first intention. Smart, it will be reassuring to note, adopted
the same policy with all seven sonnets.

V. THE ITALIAN SONNETS

MASSON raised, and rejected, the hypothesis that the Italian poems were 'written at different times and not all relating to the same object'. Preferring the alternative, that 'they are a series relating to one foreign lady, and telling the same little story', he considered two possible 'occasions', one in England, some time before the Italian tour had been thought of, the other during Milton's tour (1638–9). The argument for the first he found 'strained and unnatural' in comparison with 'the general and traditional belief that they were written in Italy'. Subsequent opinion has swung round the other way, a date between 1628 and 1630 being now very widely accepted.[1]

Most of the reasons given for the earlier date seem to me open to question: but, as they cut across the interpretation of the poems, they deserve to be heard. (i) J. H. Hanford drew on the 'biographical suggestions' in the *Elegies*:

In the envoy to Elegy VII . . . [Milton] declares that he has been freed by philosophy from his youthful errors and is henceforth proof against the tyranny of love, while in Elegy VI (written at the Christmas season of the year 1629) he seems to imply that he has bidden or is about to bid farewell to amatory themes. . . . The pieces in Latin and English which we know to have been composed in Italy or at Horton are entirely untouched by the Petrarchan mood. That Milton should be found writing to Diodati in 1638–9 in the strain which he had used a whole decade earlier is well-nigh incredible.

[1] Cf. Masson, *Life*, i. 772 ff., and revised ed., pp. 827 ff.; J. H. Hanford, 'M.'s Sonnets', and A. S. P. Woodhouse (as on p. 95 n. 2); Smart, pp. 133 ff.; D. C. Dorian, *The English Diodatis* (New Brunswick, 1950), pp. 140 ff.; Darbishire, *Poetical Works*, ii. 317–18; John Carey, 'The Date of Milton's Italian Poems' (*R.E.S.* (1963), 383–6).

Independently of Hanford, Smart pressed for the early date on other grounds. (ii) One of the sonnets was addressed to Charles Diodati, Milton's closest friend in his youth: Diodati died in London shortly before 27 August 1638 (the date of his burial), when Milton had almost certainly arrived in Florence. Rather than suppose that Milton, in ignorance of the facts, composed cheerful verses for his dead friend, Smart contended that

It is not known when Milton received the news of his friend's death; but it reached him, as he relates, when abroad; and he can hardly have been without knowledge of it during the period which he spent on Italian soil. Postal communication was then easy and familiar; letters left once a week, and, as we learn from James Howell, a practised traveller, twenty days were the usual time allowed between London and Italy.

(iii) Two of the poems afford, in Smart's view, even stronger evidence. In sonnet III

Milton compares himself to a youthful shepherdess dwelling on a rugged spot among the mountains, who tends a plant from some garden on the plain below, which cannot flourish in the bleak air, so far from its native clime: so he cultivates the flower of a foreign speech. Italian verse is the plant thus transported to an alien soil; and the rugged hill is England, where the poet writes. In the Canzone also he tells us that he is surrounded by youths and maidens who jest at his labours, and ask why he thus makes verses of love in a strange and unknown tongue — in lingua ignota e strana. It is unknown to them, for they are English and in England.

(iv) 'Milton, who keeps the chronological order in the arrangement of his sonnets, has placed the Italian poems before that on his twenty-third birthday' (Smart, p. 136).

(v) Contradicting the earlier theory that Milton's opening lines in sonnet II identified the lady as one he met in or near the vale of Reno, Smart also urged that the river and ford have 'nothing to do with his own Italian travel': they were mentioned only as clues for the name of the district in which both are located, this name being the lady's. The Reno flows through

Emilia, and 'in the eastern part of Emilia there is the most famous ford in the world — that of the Rubicon'.

(vi) John Carey supported Smart by reinterpreting the last lines of Elegy VI, in which Milton informs Diodati that he has meditated certain simple strains on 'native pipes' — '*Te quoque pressa manent patriis meditata cicutis*'. Whereas it was previously assumed that Milton referred to his own native pipes, i.e. to writing in English, Carey showed that Diodati's native pipes, i.e. Italian, could have been intended, and this would date the Italian sonnets before December 1629.

The force of the argument depends chiefly on points (ii) and (iii). Yet both are vulnerable. Against (ii) we need only quote Masson's observation, overlooked by Smart, that it is certain that Milton had not heard the news of Diodati's death some months after his leaving Florence — since he recalled in the *Epitaphium Damonis* his having looked forward to showing Diodati two 'cups' given to him by Manso at Naples.

As for (iii), the two poems paraphrased by Smart lend themselves to another explanation. Milton, surely, never meant to compare *himself* to a youthful shepherdess (though others besides Smart have read sonnet III thus, misled, perhaps, by the legend of the Lady of Christ's). Sonnet III consists of a series of parallel statements about planting and growth: (a) the shepherdess (b) waters a plant (c) on a rugged hill (d) which is an unfamiliar clime for it; (a) Love (b) quickens the new flower (c) on my swift tongue (d) which is foreign to it; (a) the Shepherd (= Him) (b) plants (c) in my slow heart and hard bosom (d) which are not good soil. The logic of the poem identifies Milton with the *rugged hill*, the *swift tongue*, the *hard bosom*, and makes Milton himself, not England, the alien soil. Smart reinforced his interpretation by translating *Fuor di* (l. 5) as *far from*, but we may take the words more literally as *outside* (i.e. the plant of Italian poetry grows outside its *genial native spring* in being transferred from the

Italians to an English poet); and the *shepherdess* we may suppose to represent Poetry or the Muse.

It is also possible to read the Canzone differently. Is the *strange and unknown tongue* 'strange' to the poet or, as Smart thought, to the bystanders who 'are English and in England' ? Here we may appeal to the preceding poem, sonnet III, where the very word *strana* of the Canzone (l. 3) was already attached to the poet and not to his countrymen — the plant being *strana e bella* (III. 3) for him, the poet's new language *strania favella* (III. 7). Perusing the Italian poems in their proper order it seems natural to accept the *strange and unknown tongue* of the Canzone as 'strange' to the poet — for is it not implied that the bystanders know Italian ? They recognise the poet's writings as *verses of love*, and they pick up his conceits : in sonnet III Milton spoke of changing the Thames for the Arno, in the Canzone they reply that *other streams, other banks await thee*. How, moreover, can the Canzone *answer for me* (l. 13) unless the poet's friends understand Italian ?

As it happens, Milton himself confessed in a letter of September 1638 his 'poverty and want of skill' in Italian, and Italian critics have always rated his grasp of their tongue, as displayed in the Italian sonnets and Canzone, less than perfect. And another confession of the poet confirms that the jesting young men and maidens of the Canzone were indeed Italian, not English. In the *Epitaphium Damonis* Milton, reminiscing about his recent stay in Florence, mentioned the poetical contests of his Italian friends and added that 'I myself even *dared* to compete' (*Ipse etiam tentare ausus sum*, l. 133). The bystanders in the Canzone ask 'why dost thou write in a strange and unknown tongue, and how dost thou dare ?' The *daring* celebrated in the *Epitaphium Damonis* most probably refers to attempts at Italian poetry, in which Milton would be at the greatest disadvantage. To return once more to Masson :

Francini's ode to him in Florence, and still more distinctly the heading of Salzilli's epigram to him in Rome, seem to imply that there had been attempts in Italian verse among those proofs of Milton's literary talents which had won him the encomiums; and we know of nothing else of the kind that he did write than precisely our present five love-sonnets, with the attached canzone.

We may now re-examine Hanford's point (i), that Milton, after rejecting 'amatory themes' in the *Elegies*, would not have relapsed a decade later. Elegy VI, let us recall, contrasts two different types of poet — one that indulges in splendid feasts and hilarious company, and one that dedicates himself to sober innocence and chastity, a bard sacred to the gods. Milton modelled himself on the second type, yet while in Italy he seems to have lived less austerely, responding, no doubt, to the Italian temperament. Hence his active participation in the contests of the convivial Italian academies which, as Masson explained, resembled the clubs or debating societies of a later age. Indeed, his tributes to the bewitching Leonora Baroni in three Latin epigrams establish that while in Italy he adopted a more Italian attitude to feminine charms: the Italian sonnets are a trifle of much the same order and, in the circumstances, would have been perfectly excusable as, at least in part, a literary exercise. In Elegy VI, we must remember, Milton renounced not only 'amatory themes' but, more generally, a way of life that allowed for love, and yet this did not prevent him from falling in love with Mary Powell.

Points (iv)–(vi) remain inconclusive. Smart himself disowned 'chronological order' elsewhere (cf. above, p. 60), and (v) and (vi) neither prove nor disprove the early date. Even if Milton had written Italian poetry when he composed Elegy VI, which is not certain, this need not have been the Italian sonnets; and, attractive as later commentators have thought Smart's conjecture about the *vale of Reno*, it rests on a textual emendation to which notice should have been drawn.[1]

[1] The only authorised texts of the sonnet, in the editions of 1645 and 1673, read not *Reno* but *Rheno*, suggesting the Rhine rather than the insignificant

While disagreement about the date and 'occasion' of the Italian poems is likely to continue, no one will seriously challenge Smart's estimate of their poetic quality. Smart admired the

Canzone and the preceding sonnet, which are perfectly fresh and original, and deal with a situation to which there is no analogy in Petrarch or any of his followers. The poet who writes in a foreign language at his lady's bidding, and because it is more the language of love than his own, introduces a new theme which is taken from immediate reality.[1]

Very probably Milton commemorated a real lady's real command, yet the 'tradition' had familiarised similar situations — the lady who orders her lover to write in her praise, and the lover who attempts poetry for the first time to please his lady (as Milton attempted *Italian* poetry). The lady's command, the tradition to which it belongs, the gentle self-mockery of the Canzone and the definitive first line of the last Italian sonnet, all help to persuade us of the young lover's simplicity, and therefore continue both the mood and the thought of sonnet I (*O Nightingale*).

Of sonnet V Smart thought less highly — 'This is the poorest of the Italian sonnets, and one of the few pieces by Milton which we might wish he had condemned to disappear'. Perhaps this was Milton's first Italian poem, a beginner's exercise in which he fell back upon clichés in order to concentrate his attention upon the language.

Reno. (Compare Keightley: 'As the name is spelt *Rheno* in the original editions, and Warton and the other critics have no note on it, we strongly suspect that they took it to be the Rhine'.) A famous ford in the Rhineland, Frankfurt, could have inspired a pun on the name of one of the poet's closest associates in Florence, Antonio *Francini*, and *Franconia*. (Frankfurt does not stand on the Rhine but, as Smart said (p. 139), Milton was 'not restricted to one river: he was more likely to mention two'.) If a relative of Francini was the *donna leggiadra* — one can only put this forward very tentatively — a late date for the Italian sonnets would inevitably follow.

[1] P. 149. Cf. Prince, pp. 97–8: 'The Italian poems as a whole, remarkable as they are, reveal themselves on consideration as a daring experiment rather than as an achieved poetic success. . . . [They] are less love-poems than slightly amorous compliments.'

COLLATION AND
COMMENTARY

I

TEXTS   (i) 1645 ; (ii) 1673. (*Not in Cambridge MS.*)

COLLATION

6   bill,] bill 1645, 1673.

11   yeer . . . yeer] 1645 ; year . . . year 1673.

12   why :] why, 1645, 1673.

COMMENTARY

As Newton already noticed in 1752, this sonnet draws on a medieval tradition, which Milton doubtless encountered in *The Cuckoo
and the Nightingale*, a poem now attributed to Sir Thomas
Clanvowe but in the seventeenth century thought to be by
Chaucer, in whose works it was printed.   According to the
tradition, it augured well for a lover to hear the nightingale, the
bird of love : but if the song of a cuckoo, the bird of hate,
sounded to him first in the spring, the lover was doomed to
disappointment for the rest of the year.

> But as I lay this other night waking
> I thought how louers had a tokening
> And among hem it was a commune tale
> That it were good to hear the Nightingale
> Rather than the leud Cuckow sing.[1]

The narrator in Clanvowe's poem goes off in search of a nightingale, but unluckily hears the cuckoo instead.   When a nightingale

[1] From Speght's *Chaucer* (1598), F. 333 ff.

also arrives the two birds begin a debate on the merits and de-
merits of love, in which the narrator naturally sympathises with
the nightingale. The cuckoo flies away, and the nightingale
thanks her supporter and promises to sing for him throughout
May.

> I thanked her, and was right well apaied
> Yea (q^d she) and be thou not dismaied
> Tho thou haue heard ye Cuckow erst than me
> For if I liue it shal amended be
> The next Maie, if I be not affraied.

The 'god of love' is an important background figure in Clanvowe's poem. It is assumed, as in Milton's concluding lines,
that he interests himself on behalf of his servants —

> For euermore loue his seruants amendeth
> And from all euill taches hem defendeth.

The poem therefore belongs to the 'courtly love' tradition.
Smart, indeed, suggested that the nightingale-cuckoo symbolism,
which he traced back to the French courtly poets, 'is not of
popular origin, but bears rather the stamp of the literary mind'.
Some folk-lore influence must however be conceded, for the
cuckoo's unpleasant character, and the related word 'cuckold',
is recorded very early.

Milton, having described the nightingale's haunt and song in
the present tense, may seem to contradict himself when he thereupon entreats it to sing for the first time that year — *Now timely
sing*. But there is no inconsistency, for the octave alludes to the
nightingale's return year after year to its old terrain, and to its
well-known habit of singing from the same tree, sometimes,
indeed, commencing its recital every night at the same time to
the minute. Nevertheless, though the present tense is later found
to be a present continuous, the opening of the sonnet suggests
a nightingale already there and audible *on yon bloomy Spray*. The
poet's vivid realisation of the bird, which is expected imminently

and already felt as a presence, conveys his excited anticipation of love.[1]

One of Milton's most sensuous and delightful poems, itself not without *liquid notes*, the sonnet may be classed as a straightforward 'complaint'. Yet the situation is seen playfully, with delicate innuendo, and therefore another interpretation seems possible. At the start all is grace and traditional courtliness : then, and only barely perceptible, a greater urgency makes itself heard. *Success in love* signifies at first glance no more than the lady's goodwill ; *amorous power*, even if granted by Jove, could be quite innocent ; Milton, however, steers towards the word *mate*, which has the primary meaning 'companion' but in its context also carries an allusion to the vulgar idea of 'mating'. Having smuggled this idea into the poem Milton ducks down again in the traditional attitude of those who abjectly *serve* and follow in love's *train*, a fitting conclusion. But perhaps one should say no more than that the *cuckoo*, the slight verbal extravagance of *the rude Bird of Hate* and *my hopeles doom*, the emphatic placing of *mate*, and the general situation, which has gone on *from yeer to yeer*, have potentially comic implications which are nevertheless kept in check : the poet expresses two moods, corresponding to the two birds, and tries to defeat the cuckoo and the mood it typifies.

Though the Italian sonnets (II–VI) perhaps date from 1638 and not from 1629 (cf. p. 76), we may tentatively accept the earlier date for O *Nightingale*. The sonnet's tone, it has been observed, resembles that of Elegies V and VII (*c.* 1628–30), where Milton welcomes the arrival of spring and of love.[2] More significantly,

---

[1] Cf. the apparent inconsistency in XX. 2 and 7 : the *ways are mire*, yet Milton also talks of the *frozen earth*. He looks forward to a winter of frozen earth, which will continue beyond the *Now* of l. 2.

[2] A. S. P. Woodhouse (cf. p. 95, n. 2) disagreed and dated O *Nightingale* in the spring of 1630, urging that the 'Petrarchianism' of this poem and of the Italian sonnets could scarcely be contemporary with the elegiac eroticism of Elegies V and VII.

M.S.—G

the sonnet was not inscribed in the Cambridge Manuscript, and therefore its composition almost certainly preceded Milton's first entries in this Manuscript (*c.* 1632–4).

1-2 *O . . . still*] Editors compare Bembo's

> O rosignuol, che 'n queste verdi fronde
> Sovra 'l fugace rio fermar ti suoli, —

and other sonnets by Della Casa, Giacomo Cenci, etc.

2 *Warbl'st*] A word much used by Milton. Compare

> nor then the solemn *Nightingal*
> Ceas'd *warbling*, but all night tun'd her *soft layes*
>
> (*P.L.* vii. 435–6)

when . . . still] Cf. the Fifth Latin Elegy:

> Iam Philomela, tuos, foliis adoperta novellis,
> Instituis modulos, dum silet omne nemus.   (Warton)

4 *jolly hours*] The πολυγηθέες Ὧραι of Homer, *Iliad*, xxi. 450 (Keightley). *Jolly*=gay.   The *Hours* were mythological female divinities, supposed to preside over the seasons: as the nightingale arrives in England in mid-April they are then about to *lead on* May.

propitious May] May was the month of love, as Shakespeare says in a song in *Love's Labour's Lost*, iv. iii. 98: 'Love, whose month is ever May'.   Cf. Milton's *Song on May Morning*.

5 *eye of Day*] It was a commonplace that the sun was the 'eye of heaven': cf. Shakespeare's *Richard II*, i. iii. 275: 'All places that the eye of heaven visits'; *Comus*, l. 978: 'Where day never shuts his eye'.

6 *shallow*] Various meanings cited in *O.E.D.* are appropriate: lacking depth; superficial; of sound: lacking resonance, 'thin'. Bacon's *Sylva* is quoted to illustrate the last: 'make the Sound perfecter, and not so Shallow and Iarring'.

'"Shallow" is a brilliant touch.   It helps keep the tone light and charming . . . and warns us not to take the poet's fear of "hopeless doom" entirely seriously' (Brooks and Hardy).

9 *rude*] uncivilized; unmusical (of sounds).

Bird of Hate] 'The cuckoo was unpropitious not only to lovers but to married people as well' (F. A. Patterson, *The Student's Milton* (New York, 1934)).

10 *ny*] The spelling is dictated by the liking for eye-rhyme (Darbishire).

13 *Whether . . . mate*] The *Muse* must be feminine, but *Love* is more probably masculine, the God of Love as in Clanvowe. Perhaps *his* = its, though this use of the word was now old-fashioned.

Some poets thought of the nightingale as masculine — e.g. Richard Barnfield in his *Ode*, l. 3 : '*Philomele* (Night-Musiques King)' — perhaps because the male is the song-bird. But Milton will scarcely have done so in a sonnet filled with classical allusions.

II

TEXTS   (i) 1645; (ii) 1673.

COLLATION

2   *Rheno*] 1645, 1673 ; *Reno* Keightley, Masson etc.

3   *Ben*] 1645; *Bene* 1673.

5   *mostrasi*] *mostra si* 1645, 1673.

6   *suoi*] 1645; *sui* 1673.

COMMENTARY

1-2 Donna . . . varco] 'The use of allusions, sometimes recondite and far-fetched, to convey the name of the person celebrated by the poet is common among Italian writers of sonnets, who love to play upon words' (Smart, quoting several examples, including one very close to Milton's sonnet by Gandolfo Porrino, a minor poet:

> O, d' ogni riverenza e d' onor degna,
>   Alma mia luce, *il cui bel nome onora*
>   L' aria, la terra, e le campagne infiora,
>   E di salir al ciel la via c' insegna,
> Luce gentil.)

7-8 E . . . s'infiora] '*La,* — *there,* — *i.e.* in the lady's eyes. These lines are no more than a texture of Petrarchian fancies, closely woven together. As Laura's poet has conceived in many places, the god of Love dwells in her eyes with his bow, and her bright glances are the arrows which are aimed at the beholder's heart. In his followers, Italian, French and English alike, the image reappears' (Smart).

10 Che . . . legno] An allusion to the story of Orpheus.

III

TEXTS (i) 1645; (ii) 1673

COLLATION

6 *Amor*] 1645; *amor* 1673.

9 *inteso,*] *inteso* 1645, 1673.

COMMENTARY

1-4 Qual . . . spera] Kuhl and Lemmi (*M.L.N.* (1924), xxxix.
49) compared Petrarch, Madrigal I :

> Ch' a me la pastorella alpestra e cruda
> Posta a bagnar un leggiadretto velo.

2 avezza] '*avezza*, more correctly *avvezza*, has given rise to
some conjecture. The adj., or syncopated p.p., derives from
avvezzare, to accustom . . . and seems here to mean "at home,
brought up there"' (Darbishire).[1]

9 dal . . . inteso] 'i.e. in a language not understood by my
countrymen in general. We are to recollect that he was writing
in Italy' (Keightley).

10 E . . . Arno] ' To change the Thames for the Arno signifies no more than to change the English language for Italian,
of which Tuscan was the classic form, here figured by the
Tuscan river ' (Smart).

CANZONE

TEXTS (i) 1645 ; (ii) 1673.

COMMENTARY

The canzone is 'a form of verse which has reached us from
Italian literature. . . . The canzone strophe consists of two parts,
the opening one being distinguished by Dante as the *fronte*, the
closing one as the *sirma*. These parts are connected by rhyme, it

---

[1] The notes on the Italian poems in Miss Darbishire's *Poetical Works* were
actually contributed by Mr John Purves.

being usual to make the rhyme of the last line of the *fronte* identical
with that of the first line of the *sirma*. In other respects the canzone has great liberty as regards number and length of lines,
arrangement of rhymes, and conduct of structure. An examination of the best Italian models, however, shows that . . . the strophe
of 14 verses is so far the most frequent that it may almost be taken
as the type. In this form it resembles an irregular sonnet'
(*Encyclopaedia Britannica*). As various commentators have observed, Milton's poem is not, strictly speaking, a canzone, but
only a canzone-stanza.

13 Canzon] 'A *canzone* ended with an envoy called the
commiato, in which the poet often addressed his poem as Milton
does here, and as Spenser did in the last stanza of his *Epithalamion*'
(Hughes).

IV

TEXTS (i) 1645; (ii) 1673.

COMMENTARY

'The young poet here retracts the opinion once expressed in
glowing Latin lines, also addressed to Diodati, in which he gives
to the maidens of England, with their clear complexion, golden
hair and rosy cheeks, the preference in beauty over all foreign
types of loveliness. . . . Having now seen an Italian face which
charms him, he assigns the palm elsewhere' (Smart, referring to
Milton's Elegy I).

1 Diodati] Cf. pp. 77, 96.

6   idea] 'The Platonic *idea* had already found a place in Petrarch' (Smart).

12   Luna] 'So again *P.L.* ii. 665 uses Virgil's figure (*Georg.* ii. 478) of the *laboring moon.* Virgil also described the moon as lured from her course by the songs of enchantresses (*Ec.* viii. 69)' (Hughes).

14   incerar . . . orecchi] '— to close the ears with wax, — an allusion to the story of Odysseus and the Sirens' (Smart).

V

TEXTS   (i) 1645 ; (ii) 1673.

COLLATION

10   *Scossomi*] *Scosso mi* 1645, 1673.

COMMENTARY

10   Scossomi . . . petto] Smart thought this almost certainly a printer's error, and proposed *Sotto il mio petto* : Kuhl and Lemmi (cf. p. 43) rejected the emendation as not idiomatic Italian.

14   Alba] 'Tasso, of whose Sonnets Milton was evidently a diligent reader, in one of them, *Quando l' Alba si leva e si rimira*, calls the lady his Aurora' (Keightley).

VI

TEXTS   (i) 1645; (ii) 1673.

COLLATION

6   *Di*] *De* 1645, 1673.

8   *e*] 1645;   *omitted* 1673.

12   *Muse*] *muse* 1645, 1673.

14   *Amor*] 1645;   *amor* 1673.

COMMENTARY

'The conflict between human love and the love of God . . . [is]
one of the fundamental themes in Petrarchan verse.   But Milton,
in adopting it from his models, has surely failed to convince us
that it faithfully reflects his own experience. . . . He expresses
himself far more effectively in the conscious nobility, the bold
self-righteousness, of sonnet VI, which in sentiment is by far the
most individual of the series' (Prince).

2   Poi . . . sono] Smart noted a reminiscence from Petrarch:

> Nè pur il mio secreto e 'l mio riposo
> Fuggo, ma più me stesso e 'l mio pensero.

'It is hard to tell whether the poet is doubtful *how* or *whether* to
flee from himself.   The former idea was a Petrarchan convention,
but the latter harmonizes better with the Stoic ideal which
colors Milton's self-portrait' (Hughes).

7-9   Quando . . . sicuro] 'Cf. Horace's just man invulnerable
against the worst that Fate can do (*Odes*, III. iii)' (Hughes).

VII

TEXTS (i) Cambridge MS., fair copy (autograph) [MS.]; (ii) 1645; (iii) 1673.

COLLATION

2 twentith] MS., 1645; twentieth 1673.

11 mean,] 1645; mean MS., 1673.

14 task-Masters] task-maisters MS.; task Masters 1645, 1673.

COMMENTARY

W. R. Parker [1] has urged that the usual date for this sonnet, December 1631, is probably mistaken. He argued that when Milton wrote 'anno aetatis 17' or 'in the 17. year' this signified 'at the age of 17' — or, in modern parlance, in the 18th year. 'Milton made this particular error in English as well as in Latin', therefore Time would not have stolen his twenty-third year till his twenty-fourth birthday.

Accepting as 'completely convincing' Parker's new date (December 1632), A. S. P. Woodhouse based upon it his important study of the sonnet.[2] Woodhouse cited J. H. Hanford's view that Elegy VI repudiated the elegiac response to life and love and was to be associated with a religious experience, the outcome of which was the *Nativity Ode* (December 1629). The elegy and ode marked a first decision, sonnet VII 'sees its final and

[1] R.E.S. (1935), xi. 276–83; but cf. Ernest Sirluck's counter-arguments in J.E.G.P. (1961), lx. 781–4.

[2] U.T.Q. (1943–4), xiii. 66–101; cf. also above, p. 87, and J. T. Shawcross, 'Milton's Decision to Become a Poet' (M.L.Q. (1963), xxiv. 21–30).

irrevocable confirmation'. Not long before writing the sonnet, in the summer of 1632, Milton had left Cambridge and retired to study for some years at his father's house at Horton.

On the threshold of the Horton period Milton's act of self-dedication required to be renewed, as it was in sonnet 7. From the determination there taken, to live and write hereafter 'As ever in my great Task-master's eye,' there is no retreat : it leaves its mark on the whole of Milton's subsequent career. And this time the decision subsumes in silence the rejection of erotic in favour of religious themes.

With what *more timely-happy spirits* did Milton compare himself ? R. M. Smith suggested Spenser, who wrote a Latin verse-letter somewhat similar to the sonnet fifty years earlier; Donald Dorian pointed to Milton's close friend Charles Diodati who, though some months the younger, was three to four years ahead of Milton both at St. Paul's School and at university.[1] Smart — rightly, I think — felt that a young poet must be intended, a contemporary of Milton whose name was already well known, and proposed Thomas Randolph.

He was Milton's contemporary at Cambridge, and had already much reputation for wit and poetic power. His brilliant little piece, *Aristippus*, had been performed at the University and published in 1630; and in 1632 he produced *The Jealous Lovers*, which was acted at Trinity before the King and Queen. . . .

If, however, we move the sonnet from December 1631 (where Smart placed it) to December 1632, we may add another reason for Parker's date, for another *timely-happy spirit* comes into the reckoning, and a more sensationally precocious one than Randolph (who was born in 1605). Abraham Cowley (born 1618) published in 1633 his *Poetical Blossoms*, a volume entered in the Stationers' Registers on 24 October 1632. We know that it was a common practice of the stationers to give books printed in the

[1] Smith, *M.L.N.* (1945), lx. 394–8; Dorian, *The English Diodatis*, pp. 122, 142–3.

last month or two of the year the date of the following year :
the S.R. entry implies that *Poetical Blossoms* appeared late in 1632,
just in time to inspire Milton's lament that he has produced no
'bud or *blossom*'.   Milton, of course, used the plural, *spirits*, and
we may therefore assume that he had in mind Cowley, Randolph,
Diodati and perhaps others.[1]

In the Cambridge Manuscript the sonnet was transcribed by
Milton at the bottom of one of the two drafts of his *Letter to a
Friend*, in which, as in the sonnet, he defends his choice of life.
The friend, apparently, disappointed by Milton's withdrawal to
further study at Horton, advised him to enter a regular profession,
preferably the Church.   Milton replied that he was not idling
away his time : learning will turn him from 'the empty and
fantastic chase of shadows and notions to the solid good flowing
from due and timely obedience to that command in the gospel
set out by the terrible seizing of him that hid the talent'.   A
'sacred reverence' restrained him, 'and religious advisement how
best to undergo, not taking thought of being late so it give
advantage to be more fit . . . Yet that you may see that I am
something suspicious of myself, and do take notice of a certain
belatedness in me, I am the bolder to send you some of my night-
ward thoughts some while since, because they come in not altogether unfitly, made up in a Petrarchian stanza.'[2]   The sonnet
followed.

Some of the words and ideas of the sonnet are reproduced in
P.L. xii. 553 ff. :

> *How soon hath* thy prediction, Seer blest,
> *Measur'd* this transient World, the Race of *time*,
> Till time stand fixt : beyond is all abyss,
> Eternitie, whose end no *eye* can reach . . .

---

[1] A. H. Nethercot (*M.L.N.* (1934), xlix. 158–62), and others, noted the possibility of an allusion to *Poetical Blossoms*, but dated the sonnet 1631, and thought
that Milton would have seen Cowley's poems in manuscript.

[2] From the second draft (Cambridge MS., p. 7), with spelling modernised.

Henceforth I learne, that to obey is best,
And love with fear the onely God, to walk
As in his presence, ever to observe
His providence . . .

1 *Time*] Behind the sonnet lies the age-old topic of 'time neglected'.

suttle] working imperceptibly or secretly. Warton compared Juvenal, *Sat*. ix. 129 : 'Dum serta, unguenta, puellas, / Poscimus, obrepit non intellecta senectus'.

2 *wing*] For the traditional image of Time's *wings* cf. *The Winter's Tale*, iv. i. 4. Cf. also *Richard III*, iii. vii. 168, 'the stealing hours of time', and v. iii. 85.

3 *My . . . career*] Cf. Job ix. 25 : 'my days . . . flee away, they see no good.'

4 *bud . . . blossom*] In Latin *flos* could = literary embellishment, and was used as a metaphor for poetry. Thus Milton's motto for *Comus*, from Virgil ('Eheu quid volui misero mihi ! *floribus* austrum / Perditus'), and *Ad Patrem*, l. 82. Whether or not Milton alludes to Cowley's *Poetical Blossoms* (cf. p. 96), he employs the same commonplace. He had, indeed, written other poems by now, notably the *Nativity Ode*, but had not yet published in his own name (cf. *shew'th*, l. 4) — except for *On Shakespeare* (printed in the Second Folio of 1632), a purely complimentary poem. That his failure to publish weighed on him is confirmed by the *Letter to a Friend*, where he hints that he hopes not to live in 'prolonged obscurity', since there is such a thing as desire of 'immortall fame seated in the brest of every true scholar which all make hast to by the readiest ways of publishing'.

5-6 *Perhaps . . . near*] 'He was so fair that they called him the Lady of Christ's College' says Aubrey of Milton at this period

(*Lives*, p. 3). Later, in the *Second Defence*, Milton claimed that most people thought him ten years younger than he was.

deceive] prove false.

9 *less . . . more*] A not unusual phrase at this time, found in the Bible (1 Samuel xxii. 15, xxv. 36), and elsewhere in Milton.

9-12 *Yet . . . Heav'n*] Cf. Pindar's Fourth Nemean Ode: 'But whatsoever merit King Fate has given to me, I well know that Time in its course will accomplish what is destined' (L. Campbell, *Classical Review*, October 1894).

10-11 *It . . . lot*] In 1645 and 1673 there is a comma after *eev'n*; in the MS. there is no punctuation. The comma suggests 'It shall be always in strictest measure evenly-paced, proceeding to that same lot'; the MS. suggests '. . . in strictest measure, even to that same lot'.

13-14 *All . . . eye*] There is no punctuation in the MS. The 1645 edition has the two commas which, Woodhouse thought (*loc. cit.*), reduce the lines 'to something between redundancy and nonsense'. Accordingly, Woodhouse changed the first comma to a colon, and explained 'All [that matters] is: whether I have grace to use it so, as ever [conscious of being] in my great Task-master's [enjoining] eye'.[1]

Donald Dorian (*The Explicator* (1949), viii. item 10) interprets the line to mean, 'All time is, if I have grace to use it so, as eternity in God's sight'. This seems a more likely explanation, for Milton resorts to two antitheses traditional in the sonnet, the second member of each antithesis being less explicit than the first: Time *versus* Eternity, Appearance *versus* Reality. After the 'flying Time' topic one expects the thought to turn to Eternity (as often in Shakespeare), just as one expects the assertion of 'false Appear-

---

[1] Cf. K. Svendsen's paraphrase: 'All that matters is whether I have grace to use my ripeness in accordance with the will of God as one ever in His sight' (*The Explicator* (1949), vii. item 53).

ances' (l. 5 etc.) to lead to a discovery of 'Reality'. These expectations are met in the two concluding lines, in which Milton discards Time ('All is . . . timeless [*or* ever-present, *or* eternal] in my great Taskmaster's eye'), and thus consoles himself for Time's apparent vagaries, since the *eye* becomes a symbol of God's omniscience and an assurance that false appearances cannot deceive. In poetry about poetry (cf. l. 4) it was of course commonplace from the ancients onwards to defy Time.

Cf. also 2 Chron. xvi. 9: 'the eyes of the Lord run to and fro throughout the whole earth, to shew himself strong in the behalf of them whose heart is perfect toward him', Ps. xxxiii. 18: 'the eye of the Lord is upon them that fear him', xxxiv. 15, and Milton's account of his continental tour: 'I lived free and untouched of all defilement . . . having it ever in my thought, that if I could escape the eyes of men, I certainly could not escape the eyes of God' (*Pro Se Defensio*, *C.M.* ix. 179, a passage repeated almost word for word from the *Second Defence*, viii. 127). J. M. French has shown (*P.M.L.A.* (1938), liii. 363–6) that the 'NB' placed opposite 2 Chron. xvi. 9 in Milton's family Bible is probably in the poet's hand.

13 *grace*] After what precedes, an allusion to *grace* and *works*. Milton takes the Protestant view that works without faith and grace are valueless.

14 *As . . . eye*] *Th' Eternal eye* (*P.L.* v. 711, x. 5), not to be confused with *the eye of Day* (cf. p. 88), stands for God's omniscience and providence. It is emblematically represented on, for example, the title-page of Raleigh's *History of the World*, 1614 (cf. the Oxford *Jonson* (1947), viii. 177).

task-Masters] In the Bible the Egyptians set taskmasters over the people of Israel 'to afflict them with their burdens' (Exod. i. 11 etc.). Milton borrowed the word not to complain of a harsh overseer but to suggest that he himself may have a special task, as a poet.

VIII

TEXTS   (i) Cambridge MS., fair copy (scribal) [MS.]; (ii) 1645;
(iii) 1673.

TITLE   On his dore when yᵉ Citty expected an assault
(MS.; *deleted title*); When the assault was intended to yᵉ
Citty (MS.; *inserted title, autograph*); 1642 (MS.; *marginal note,
deleted*).

COLLATION

3 If deed of honour did thee ever please] 1673 ; If ever deed
of honour did thee please MS., 1645.

11 Temple] temple' MS.

COMMENTARY

At the start of the Civil War (22 August 1642) a Royalist move
against London was expected, and might have been successful if
swiftly executed after the Battle of Edgehill (23 October). The
king's army sacked Brentford (12 November), but halted next
day when 24,000 men blocked its way at Turnham Green:
outnumbered, the Royalists withdrew, and London was not
assaulted.

Milton's sonnet is usually said to have been written on 12
or 13 November, when Londoners worked feverishly, digging
trenches and barricading the streets, to prepare for the enemy.
I find this hard to believe, for several reasons. (i) Royalist atrocities against Parliamentarians were widely publicised in the autumn

of 1642:[1] Milton writes detachedly, playfully, as if for a less serious situation. (ii) Yet Milton, of all people, could scarcely think of himself as detached, being already notorious as the author of some of the most bitter anti-Royalist pamphlets of his day. (iii) In any case, he was not the man to ask for special favours in a situation like that of 1642. Throughout his life he remained undaunted and intransigent in the face of his various enemies.[2]

It has been observed by others that in the circumstances of 1642 the sonnet is a little odd.

The poet seems to bow his head before the conqueror, and to offer his music as the price of leniency, with a Greek submission to the Fates strangely at variance with his habitual temper.[3]

What has not been observed is the tenuousness of the evidence for 1642. The date was actually deleted in the Cambridge Manuscript, but the significance of this afterthought has not been recognised.

Several sonnets in the Manuscript had their titles and dates scored out, not because these were erroneous but because of a change of policy concerning the printing of superscriptions (cf. p. 72). The editors naturally accepted the truth of the facts thus deleted, but failed to notice that sonnet VIII requires a different explanation. For the date and title of this sonnet were not crossed out together, as a matter of policy: Milton left his title and only deleted the date. We must suppose, therefore, that he came to recognise that the date was wrong. Were it contemporary with the sonnet's composition this would be surprising: but as the

---

[1] E.g. in J. Goodwin's *Anti-Cavalierisme* ('Pleading . . . for the suppressing of that Butcherly brood of Cavaliering Incendiaries, who are now hammering England'); *A Wonderfull Deliverance* ('Declaring how many Troopes of the Cavaliers came against [Draiton] . . . with an intent to have plundered it and put the inhabitants to the Sword, Men, Women, and Children') — both of October 1642. (*Thomason Tracts*, E. 123.)

[2] Cf. his enthusiastic swordsmanship, his behaviour at Rome when threatened with danger (*C.M.* viii. 61, 125), and his outspoken publications just before the Restoration.   [3] Moody, p. 73.

scribal copy accompanied by the date seems to belong to a later period, Milton could easily have mistaken the year.[1]

Placed in 1642, the sonnet is puzzling. Not so if we relate it to another intended assault, which threw Londoners into an uproar early in May 1641 :

a treacherous Design was set on foot, not without the Participation of the King, as appear'd under his own Hand, to bring up the English Army, and by Force to dissolve the Parliament; the Plunder of *London* being promised to the Officers and Souldiers as a Reward for that Service: This was confessed by the Lord *Goring*, Mr. *Piercy*, and others.[2]

It seems unlikely that Milton, a marked man and a declared enemy in 1642, should expect or ask for special consideration — which the sonnet certainly suggests, though perhaps never intended as a practical expedient. In May 1641, on the other hand, he had not published a single pamphlet against the king's party, the Civil War had not yet begun, and rumoured 'army-plots' could therefore be viewed with the playful detachment that is so curious a feature of the sonnet.

1 *Colonel*] A trisyllable.

Knight in Arms] Cf. *Richard II*, I. iii. 26: 'Marshal, ask yonder knight in arms, Both who he is and why he cometh hither' (Warton).

[1] For Milton's mistaken dates for his poems cf. Hanford, *Handbook*, pp. 138–139, 146. I think the version of VIII in the Cambridge MS. a late one since (i) the title is retrospective; (ii) the sonnet itself either dates from 1642 or (as I believe) from 1641; (iii) VIII was entered in the MS. by a scribe, whose presence is best explained as a result of Milton's alarm in 1644 (cf. p. 172) at his failing sight. If I am right it appears that the *autograph* versions of IX and X, written below the *scribal* version of VIII on the same page, either have 1644 as their *terminus a quo*, or (more probably) are also late copies. It would follow from the latter view that Milton tinkered with IX long after finishing it — which, of course, he is known to have done with other poems. (Cf. p. 195.) The example of eye-skip in X. 3 suggests that X is a copy.

[2] Edmund Ludlow, *Memoirs* (Switzerland, 1698, 2 vols.), i. 15; cf. Masson, *Life*, ii. 183–4.

2 *these . . . dores*] Because Milton's house was just outside the city-wall (Masson, *Life*, ii. 204–7). Hence, perhaps, the allusion to *th' Athenian Walls*.

3 *ever*] The change in the 1673 ed. looks deliberate.

5 *charms*] Possibly a pun on charm = song, as in *P.L.* iv. 642 : 'charm of earliest Birds'.

8 *clime*] a belt of the earth's surface contained between two parallels of latitude (*O.E.D.*).

the . . . circle] Cf. *P.L.* iv. 578 : 'Amid the Suns bright circle where thou sitst'. The *circle* probably refers to the sun's shape rather than the older view of its course round the earth (for which cf. *P.L.* iv. 592 ff., v. 558, vii. 370 etc.).

9 *Lift . . . Bowre*] The pike, a short *spear*, was still widely used by infantry at this time. And Milton, who liked to think of himself as one withdrawn in the bowers of the Muses,[1] lived from 1640 to 1645 in what might be called a bower — 'a pretty Garden-House', as his nephew described it, 'a House of the Muses'.[2] Neither *spear* nor *Bowre* was therefore entirely divorced from the facts. Milton, however, chose his words so as to measure the present against the heroic past, the gap between the two no doubt affording him as much wry amusement as the image of a *spear* lifted against a *Bowre*. In the next line, where he compares a petty commander with the *great Emathian Conqueror*, his sardonic implications become even more clear.

10 *The . . . Conqueror*] Alexander the Great. Emathia was a district of Macedon, but the name was used poetically for Macedon itself. Ovid speaks of Alexander as *dux Emathius*. During Alexander's absence from Greece the Thebans rose in revolt against him : he reappeared, and stormed their city. The inhabi-

---

[1] Letter to Gill, July 1628 : 'quasi Claustris Musarum delitescere'.
[2] *Lives*, pp. 62, 67.

tants were slaughtered or sold into slavery, and Thebes was razed to the ground. 'It is said that Alexander spared only the house once occupied by Pindar, and showed favour to his descendants; but the story rests on doubtful authority. In literature it became a subject of familiar allusion' (Smart).

11 *Temple . . . Towre*] 'A frequent combination in the old metrical romances' (Warton, quoting examples, and also *P.R.* iii. 268, iv. 34).

12-14 *And . . . bare*] 'Plutarch relates, that when the Lacedemonian general Lysander took Athens, it was proposed in a council of war entirely to raze the city. . . . But during the debate, at a banquet of the chief officers, a certain Phocian sung some fine anastrophics from a chorus of the *Electra* of Euripides, which so affected the hearers that they declared it an unworthy act to reduce a place, so celebrated for the production of illustrious men, to total ruin' (Warton).

12 *the . . . air*] the repetition of the air.

13 *sad*] Taken by some to refer to Electra, by others to Euripides.

IX

TEXTS (i) Cambridge MS., corrected fair copy (autograph) [MS.]; (ii) 1645; (iii) 1673.

COLLATION

5 with *Ruth*] MS., 1673; the *Ruth* 1645.

6 hast,] 1645, 1673; hast; MS.

7 growing vertues] MS., 1645, 1673. (MS. *orig.* blooming vertues *altered to* prospering vertue *altered to* growing vertues.)

their] 1645, 1673 ; thir MS.

13 Passes . . . night] MS., 1645, 1673. (MS. *orig.* opens the dore of Bliss, that hovre of night, *altered to* passes to bliss at ye midd watch ⟨ . . ⟩ night *and 'watch' then altered to 'howr'.*)

COMMENTARY

It was once conjectured that the 'Lady' may have been 'one of Dr. *Davis's* Daughters, a very Handsome and Witty Gentlewoman' whom, according to Edward Phillips, Milton hoped to marry when his first wife in effect deserted him.[1] Smart, however, thought it

not in any way a love sonnet. The poet is addressing a girl who is still very young — *in the prime of earliest youth*, with the kindness and encouragement of an elder friend. . . . The girl to whom he speaks had been the subject of reproof or asperity, and had made the poet the confidant of her distress. . . . That some one 'fretted at her growing virtues' can only mean that in a narrow spirit she had been thought precocious and priggish.

As Milton's two first lines could refer *back* to the lady's earliest youth she need not have been as 'very young' as Smart held. And there are indications that those who fretted at her were irritated by something other than a priggish temper. The stories of Mary and of Ruth are both related to the coming of Christ's Kingdom,[2] as is the parable of the Wise and Foolish Virgins : to care for one's lamp meant to live a truly Christian life and thus to win *entrance* into the Church, of which Christ is the *Bridegroom*.

Since the sonnet was written by a Puritan it seems reasonable to assume that Milton applauds the lady's Puritan inclinations, *they that overween* and *fret their spleen* being most probably, in

---

[1] *Lives*, p. 66; cf. Masson, *Life*, iii. 435 ff.
[2] Cf. Brooks and Hardy, pp. 158–9.

view of her age, her own family. If so, a particular young lady,
who played an important part in Milton's life, very neatly fits
the situation.

Mary Powell, the poet's first wife, 'used to a great House, and
much Company and Joviality',[1] had to abandon her former style
of living when she married a Puritan. After the event, apparently,
she found 'a Philosophical Life' not to her taste, but before
marrying her Milton no doubt supposed her sympathetic to his
stricter ways. In *The Doctrine and Discipline of Divorce* he complained 'that the bashfull mutenes of a virgin may oft-times hide'
her real feelings, and that inexperienced young men are 'not so
quick-sighted' as to guess them.[2] Some of his complaints in the
pamphlet clearly sprang from his personal misadventures. It
seems likely, therefore, that he deceived himself as to Mary
Powell's inclinations during their very brief courtship of one
month — an inference borne out by the fact that she left him
after 'a Month or thereabout' and returned to her parents.

If Mary Powell, in the weeks before her marriage, was the
'virtuous young lady' of the sonnet, she would fit the facts in
other respects. Whatever her age, the 'young lady' must have
been considerably younger than the poet. In 1642, the year to
which his marriage is now assigned,[3] Milton was thirty-three and
his bride sixteen. Comparison 'with *Mary* and with Ruth' (l. 5)
would be peculiarly appropriate. And the oblique allusions to
marriage would have special point if the poet and 'Lady' were
themselves about to marry.

1 *Lady,*] A not uncommon opening for sonnets, found in
Constable's *Diana* ('Lady, in beauty and in favour rare'), Tofte's
Laura, etc. *Signora* and *Madame* similarly opened Italian and
French sonnets.

[1] *Lives*, pp. 64 ff.   [2] *C.M.* III ii. 394.
[3] Cf. B. A. Wright's articles on 'Milton's First Marriage' in *M.L.R.* xxvi
and xxvii (1931, 1932), and *Lives*, pp. xl ff.

1-4 *Lady . . . Truth*] 'The contrast between the easy way of
vice and the toilsome upward path of virtue is familiar in ancient
literature. . . . But Milton blends the classical image of virtue as
a steep mountain with that of the Gospel, — "Wide is the gate
and broad is the way, that leadeth to destruction . . . and narrow
is the way which leadeth unto life, and few there be that find it"'
(Matt. vii. 13, 14).

'It is less evident why the broad way to destruction is also
called *green*. The expression is not in the Bible, but is apparently
of medieval origin' (Smart). From one of Daniel's *Delia* sonnets
the implications of *green* are easily inferred :

> A modest maid, decked with a blush of honour,
> Whose feet do tread *green paths of youth and love.*

3 *eminently*] in an elevated position (on the hill of truth) ; in
an eminent degree, notably.

4 *heav'nly Truth*] truth in heavenly matters.

5 *The . . . part*] 'Mary hath chosen that good part, which shall
not be taken away from her' (Luke x. 42). Mary is compared
with her sister, Martha, and Ruth with her sister-in-law, Orpah
(Ruth i. 14), Mary and Ruth representing Christian womanhood.

The phrase 'the better part', instead of the Bible's 'that good
part', seems to have been widely used : cf. Della Casa's sonnet
to a friend who entered a monastery — 'Eletto ben hai tu la
miglior parte' ;[1] Richard Baxter's *Christian Directory* (1673), p.
290 : '*Mary* . . . chose the better part, which shall not be taken
from her'.

7 *fret*] Suggested by the behaviour of Martha, who 'was cum-
bered about much serving, and came to him, and said, Lord,
dost thou not care that my sister hath left me to serve alone ?'

8 *ruth*] compassion. As Todd noted, 'pity and ruth' was a

---

[1] 'Thou hast indeed chosen the better part.' Quoted by Prince, p. 16.

not uncommon phrase in earlier poetry. The identical rhyme (Ruth — ruth) would not have offended in Milton's day, since even the greatest poets (Spenser and Shakespeare) sometimes rhymed in this way.

9-14 *Thy . . . pure*] Alluding to the parable of the ten virgins (Matt. xxv. 1 ff.) 'which took their *lamps*, and went forth to meet the *bridegroom*. And five of them were *wise*, and five were foolish.' The wise ones took oil for their lamps, the foolish ones did not. 'And *at midnight* there was a cry made, Behold, the *bridegroom* cometh . . .' The foolish virgins had to leave to buy oil, the wise ones '*went in* with him to the marriage: and the door was shut'.

10 *deeds . . . light*] Cf. John iii. 19–21 : 'every one that doeth evil hateth the light, . . . lest his deeds should be reproved. But he that doeth truth cometh to the light, that his deeds may be made manifest.'

11 *Hope . . . shame*] Cf. Rom. v. 3–5 : 'we glory in tribulations also : knowing that tribulation worketh patience ; And patience, experience ; and experience, hope : And hope maketh not ashamed . . .'

12 *Thou*] *Thou* is emphatically placed, to contrast with *they* (l. 6).

feastfull] festive.

13 *bliss*] the perfect joy of heaven ; the beatitude of departed souls. Hence, the place of bliss, paradise, heaven (*O.E.D.*).

14 *entrance*] Cf. ll. 9–14, note, and John x. 9 : 'I am the door : by me if any man enter in, he shall be saved'.

X

TEXTS (i) Cambridge MS., fair copy (autograph) [MS.]; (ii)
1645; (iii) 1673.

TITLE   To yᵉ Lady Margaret Ley MS.

COLLATION

3 liv'd in] MS., *etc.* (MS. *orig.* Left them).

8 Kill'd] 1673, MS.; Kil'd 1645.

COMMENTARY

It is usually assumed that this sonnet dates from the period of
Milton's wife's absence in Oxford (1642–6). Edward Phillips
wrote —

Our Author, now as it were a single man again, made it his chief
diversion now and then in an Evening to visit the Lady *Margaret Lee*,
daughter to the —— *Lee*, Earl of *Marlborough*, Lord High Treasurer
of *England*, and President of the Privy Councel to King *James* the
First. This Lady being a Woman of great Wit and Ingenuity, had
a particular Honour for him, and took much delight in his Company,
as likewise her Husband Captain *Hobson*, a very Accomplish'd Gentleman ; and what Esteem he at the same time had for Her, appears by
a Sonnet he made in praise of her, to be seen among his other Sonnets
in his Extant Poems.[1]

As I understand him, Phillips merely cited the sonnet as a general
illustration of his uncle's regard for Lady Margaret : that Milton's

---

[1] *Lives*, p. 64. The Hobsons were near neighbours of Milton in Aldersgate
St. (Smart, pp. 62, 160), but, while it is possible that neither Hobson nor Lady
Margaret lived near Milton before their marriage in 1641, there is no reason to
suppose that their friendship with him resulted from their living in the same
street.

friendship with Lady Margaret only began after his wife's departure, or that the sonnet was written after that event, is by no
means indicated. (The phrase *at the same time* underlines an antithesis, and surely carries no temporal implications.) Indeed, as
W. R. Parker has observed,[1] Milton's manuscript title, using
Lady Margaret's maiden name, obliges us to consider a date for
the sonnet prior to December 1641, when she became Lady
Margaret Hobson, the wife of John Hobson of Ningwood in
the Isle of Wight (cf. also ll. 5–6, note).

1   *that*] 'Note repetition (1, 5, 6, 8) of *that* = "the well-known"
(Lat. *ille*)' (Verity).

good Earl] James Ley was born around 1552, the younger son
of a Wiltshire squire. He studied law, was appointed by King
James to an Irish Chief Judgeship (1604), was knighted (1609),
baroneted (1620), made Chief Justice of the Court of the King's
Bench (1621), and Lord High Treasurer (1624). Charles I raised
him to the Earldom of Marlborough, but, finding him less useful
than he wished as Lord Treasurer, shelved him into the less
important office of Lord President of the Council (Masson, *Life*,
iii. 57; *Dictionary of National Biography*).

Though Fuller described him as 'a person of great gravity,
ability, and integrity' (*Worthies*), both Ley's *goodness* and his
integrity are open to suspicion. Sir James Whitelocke thought
him crafty and underhand, and recorded in 1627 that 'he was
wont to be called "Vulpone", and I think he as well deservethe
it now as ever'. Ley is also said to have offered £10,000 for the
attorney-generalship, when it fell vacant in 1617 (Edward Foss,
The Judges of England).

[1] *P.M.L.A.* (1958), lxxiii. 200. It is admittedly an open question whether
every lady with a courtesy title adopted her husband's name at this time. Some
did (e.g. Lady Dryden); but even if Lady Margaret also did so, Milton, sup-
posing he wrote the sonnet after her marriage, may still have preferred to call
her by her maiden name in order to identify *that good Earl*, her father.

3 *unstain'd . . . fee*] The most sensational trial in Ley's life-time dealing with bribe-taking by judges was Bacon's (1621). Ley presided at it and pronounced sentence — and Milton perhaps alludes to this (M. H. Nicolson, *John Milton* (1964), p. 146).

4 *more . . . content*] Either 'more content with himself as a private person', or 'more content with himself for not taking bribes'.

5-6 *Till . . . him*] In *Eikonoklastes* Milton discussed King Charles's several dissolutions of Parliament, which were an 'affront and indignity put upon the House' (*C.M.* v. 76). That of 1629 'was accompanied by tumultuous scenes, and marked a complete breach between Charles I and the Parliamentary leaders, and the beginning of eleven years of arbitrary government. At the last sitting the Speaker, on rising to adjourn the House, was forcibly held down in his chair by Holles and Valentine, while a resolution protesting against the policy of the king was adopted. . . . From Milton's allusion it appears that the news of these events reached Lord Marlborough on his deathbed, and was believed by those about him to have hastened his end' (Smart, adding that he knew of no confirmation of this account of Ley's death — which Milton no doubt heard from Lady Margaret).

Perhaps we may regard *the sad breaking of that Parlament* as a topical allusion. The king's bad habit of breaking (dissolving) his Parliaments was brought to an end in May 1641, when he assented to a bill enacting that the existing Parliament should not be dissolved except with its own consent (Masson, *Life*, ii. 187). This important constitutional measure came in the same year as the Earl of Marlborough's first posthumous publication, for which Milton may have written his sonnet as 'complimentary verses' (cf. p. 49).

6-8 *as . . . eloquent*] Athens and Thebes were overwhelmed by the Macedonians at the battle of Chaeronea (338 B.C.), and lost their independence. The orator Isocrates, according to a tradition familiar in Milton's day but now regarded as doubtful, died from grief four days after the battle, in his ninety-eighth year, — 'as Ley's death followed exactly four days after the dissolution of Parliament on 10 March 1629' (Pattison).

6 *dishonest*] shameful.

9 *later born*] Not literally true, as Milton was born in 1608, unless *flourish* = 'to be in one's bloom or prime' (*O.E.D.* 4).

10 *you*] In all his other sonnets Milton used the second person singular : he switched to the plural form here for the sake of the rhyme.

13 *That . . . true*] Suggested by the fact that Ley was a *judge*, and had to evaluate evidence ?

14 Margaret] 'At least three Italian sonnets close with a similar line. Cf. "Come virtù di stella Margherita" (Dante), "Preziosa e mirabil Margherita" (Tasso), "Preziosa e celeste Margherita" (Claudio Tolomei)' (Smart).

XI

TEXTS (i) Cambridge MS., ? fair copy (autograph) [MS. 1];
(ii) Cambridge MS., fair copy (scribal) [MS. 2]; (iii) 1673.

TITLE On the detraction wch follow'd upon my writing certain treatises MS. 1 *deleted*; On the detraccon which followed upon my writeng certaine treatises MS. 2; On the same. 1673. (*Numbered* '11' *in MSS.* 1 + 2, *but in* MS. 2 '11' *was changed to*

'12'. *In 1673 this sonnet was numbered* 'XII', *and sonnet XII became*
'XI').

COLLATION

4   Cuckoes] MS. 2, 1673 ; buzzards MS. 1.

10   And . . . free] MS. 1 *etc.* (MS. 1 *orig.* And hate the truth
wherby they should be free).
Milton's autograph spellings (MS. 1) *included* : thir, clogs, dogs,
frogs, hogs, thir, Truth, farr, roav.

COMMENTARY

When Mary Powell deserted him in 1642, after only a month or
so of married life, Milton 'thought upon a Divorce, that hee
might bee free to marry another. . . . The lawfulness and expedi-
ence of this . . . had upon full consideration & reading good
Authors bin formerly his Opinion'.[1]   To persuade others to
accept his opinion he published, in fairly rapid succession, *The
Doctrine and Discipline of Divorce* (1643 ; second edition, 'revis'd
and much augmented', Jan.–Feb. 1644); *The Judgment of Martin
Bucer* (July 1644) ; and *Tetrachordon* and *Colasterion* (both in
March 1645).

It was necessary to write so many pamphlets because the
Presbyterians, his former allies (cf. p. 35), disowned Milton's
radical proposals, and indeed denounced him as one of the most
abominable of the new 'sectaries'. Herbert Palmer seems to
have been the first to do so publicly, in a sermon preached before
both Houses of Parliament on 13 August 1644, in which he outlined the undesirable consequences of Toleration — one being a
new theory of divorce 'of which a wicked book is abroad and
uncensured, though deserving to be burnt, whose Author hath
been so impudent as to set his name to it and dedicate it to your-

---

[1] *Lives*, p. 23, from the 'anonymous biographer'.

selves'. Others who snapped at Milton included Prynne (Sept.
1644), and Daniel Featley (Jan. 1645), who deplored 'a Tractate
on Divorce, in which the bonds of marriage are let loose to
inordinate lust and putting away wives for many other causes
besides that which our Saviour only approveth, viz. in case of
Adultery'.[1] These men made the *barbarous noise* that environed
Milton. He, in turn, aimed a personal slap at every one of his
persecutors in his later divorce pamphlets — which inclines me
to think that a similar personal animus powerfully influenced the
writing of some of the sonnets. This was Masson's view, from
which Smart dissented.[2]

In addition to the divorce tracts the *certain treatises* mentioned
in Milton's cancelled title could designate *Areopagitica* (Nov. 1644),
since this 'speech for the liberty of unlicensed printing', which
itself gave rise to new *detraction*, was written after Milton ran
into trouble for the unlicensed printing of *The Doctrine and
Discipline of Divorce*. According to Masson 'there can be little
doubt that the Assembly divines and the London clergy generally', together with the leaders of the Stationers' Company, stirred
up this new trouble [3] — in short, in the argument about divorce
and in that about licensing the enemy was the same. As I have
suggested (p. 33), Milton neatly connected the two issues and
turned their own words against the Presbyterians in *Licence they
mean when they cry libertie*.

What enormities had Milton advocated to antagonise the
Presbyterians as he did ? By modern Protestant standards his
central contention seems less revolutionary than in his own day.
He urged that all forms of incompatibility destroy the mutual
love that is the basis of marriage, and should be recognised as an
adequate reason for divorce : husband and wife would otherwise

---

[1] Cf. Masson, *Life*, iii. 262–3, 298–9, 300–1.
[2] Cf. p. 198, and below.
[3] Masson, *Life*, iii. 273, 293 ff.

be 'two carkasses chain'd unnaturally together; or as it may happ'n, a living soule bound to a dead corps.' [1]

Incompatibility is now taken more seriously than in the seventeenth century. We are, consequently, tempted to smile at the Presbyterians, and to say that Milton was quite simply ahead of his time. It should then be added that he also proposed divorce by mutual consent (with, of course, certain safeguards) — and that, though 'public morality' now moves in the same direction, neither Protestant churches nor civil codes in Protestant countries have yet gone to this extreme. For a Christian society Milton's were very radical views indeed. Furthermore, it was inevitable that in an age when free love was allegedly a principle with various 'Christian' communities, Familists, Anabaptists, etc., the 'Divorcers' should be associated with these discreditable minorities, and not given a fair hearing.

Contemptuous though he no doubt was of most of his fellow 'sectaries', Milton must have resented attacks on dissenters in general, being himself implicated. The Presbyterians pointed to the extraordinary multiplication of sects, and asked where this would end: the 'sectaries', they held, were light-headed innovators whose clamouring had brought about a second Babel.

They all pretend to set the right bound, build the Lords house; but it is *Babel*, not *Bethel*, if wee may guesse by the division of their languages. . . .[2]

Just as commonplace was the dismissal of the sectaries as mere vermin :

all manner Sectaries creepe forth, and multiplie, as frogs, and flies, and vermine in the Spring; and there *is variance, hatred, emulation, wrath, strife, sedition, heresies, envyings, revilings, and the like.*[3]

---

[1] *C.M.* III ii. 478.
[2] N. Hardy, *The Arraignment of Licentious Liberty* (1647), p. 14.
[3] John Ward, *God Iudging among the Gods* (1645), p. 31.

Writing of the *barbarous noise* of his 'verminous' opponents (*owls, frogs, etc.*) Milton therefore turned the Presbyterians' jargon against themselves, a trick to which he resorted again in *Licence they mean when they cry libertie.*

There may also be a topical innuendo in *casting Pearl to Hoggs.* The House of Lords ordered Mr Justice Reeves and Mr Justice *Bacon* to examine Milton in December 1644, after he had flouted the regulations about book-licensing.[1] Another *Bacon*, a member of the Commons, was put in charge of a Parliamentary committee 'to prepare and bring in an Ordinance for the Prevention of the Growth and Spreading of Heresies',[2] and on 2 September 1646 presented an ordinance which made it a felony to utter theological views diverging from those laid down by Parliament, and imposed the death penalty on 'heretics' who refused to renounce their errors — an ordinance designed to crush Independence, from which Bacon won much publicity.[3]

Masson dated sonnet XI and its companion-piece, sonnet XII, between October 1645 and January 1646.[4] Others place the poems in 1646 or 1647 — a more likely date, at least for XII, a rough draft of which follows in the Cambridge Manuscript after XIV, since XIV cannot be earlier than December 1646. That XI follows XIII in the Manuscript may not be so significant, for, though XIII is headed 9 February 1645/6, XI looks like a fair copy and could therefore have been written down elsewhere before being entered in the Cambridge Manuscript.

1 *cloggs*] 'literally means weights or encumbrances put upon beasts to prevent them from straying' (Moody).

2 *antient libertie*] 'i.e. before divorce was restrained by the

---

[1] Cf. l. 11, *Licence they mean*, and Masson, *Life*, iii. 295.
[2] *Journals of the House of Commons*, 29 April 1646.
[3] Cf. *An Ordinance Presented . . . by Mr. Bacon* (1646), (an Independent attack on the Ordinance).   [4] *Life*, iii. 460.

canon law' (Pattison). Or was Milton thinking of the 'three species of liberty' mentioned in the *Second Defence* ?

3 *barbarous*] Cf. XII. 10–11, n.

4 *Owles . . . Doggs*] 'all with ugly voices, and each one traditionally a symbol: the owl of ignorance, the cuckoo of ingratitude and vanity, the ass, of stupidity and obstinacy, the ape of empty mockery, and the dog of quarrelsomeness' (Nicolson, p. 165).

5-7 *As . . . fee*] When Latona, with her new-born twins, Apollo and Diana, fled from the wrath of Juno, she came to Lycia and, being thirsty, wished to drink from a lake of clear water. Some countrymen who were there stopped her; when she pleaded with them, they added threats and abusive language. As a punishment, Latona changed them into frogs (Ovid, *Metamorphoses*, vi. 331 ff.).

W. R. Parker has suggested that *Tetrachordon* and *Colasterion* are referred to. 'These non-identical twins, both with Greek names, were "born" or published on the same day, 4 March 1645, according to Thomason. . . . The rude tormentors of the mythological twins were "transformed to frogs" by Jove. The animal noises which greeted his own newly-born twins, Milton humorously suggests, may have resulted from a similar metamorphosis' (*The Explicator* (1949), viii. item 3). If Parker is right, the Latona allusion would be appropriate in another way. Latona's twins had a difficult birth, because of Juno's hostility (cf. Ovid). Milton's two pamphlets appeared two months after the Stationers' Company (instigated by the Assembly of Divines) complained to the House of Lords of 'the frequent printing of scandalous Books' by 'Jo. Milton'. The Lords at once ordered an examination of Milton (28 December 1644). As the stationers had previously complained of him to the Commons (August 1644), no printer would be anxious to take on more divorce tracts by Milton in 1645. Neither *Tetrachordon* nor *Colasterion* gave a printer's name in the imprint — so there can be little doubt that the 'twin' pamphlets had a difficult birth as well.

Thomas E. Maresca has also observed that Renaissance writers found two meanings in the Latona-myth that throw light on the sonnet : (i) Latona represents *iniuriarum oblivionem*; (ii) Latona represents Faith or the Scripture, and the rustics are vile and impatient persons justly punished by God (*M.L.N.* (1961), lxxvi. 491-4).

5 *Hinds*] rustics, boors; with a further suggestion of the animal-nature of his enemies.

8 *But . . . Hoggs*] 'Give not that which is holy unto the dogs, neither cast ye your pearls before swine, lest they trample them under their feet, and turn again and rend you' (Matt. vii. 6).

Since there may be a personal hit in *Hoggs* (cf. p. 117), it should be added that *Pearl* could be another topical allusion. John Lilburne's *Pearle in a Dounghill* (1646, dated 'June 30th' by Thomason) gave great offence to the Presbyterians as an opposition pamphlet, and might therefore be cited approvingly by Milton. If *Pearle* appeared too late for such an allusion — as I am inclined to think — it is still interesting, in its closeness to sonnet XI, as an index of floating ideas, upon which Milton also draws. Lilburne is called 'a man that hath discovered more of the *liberties of England*, then any one man alive'. The author deplores that, 'in a time so zealously pretending to reformation', so much should be left unreformed, e.g. 'That the Presse should be stopt . . . admitting only what *appointed* Lycencers shall allow'. He asks 'For what it is so much precious blood hath been spilt, so many Families wasted, so much treasure consumed', and believes that the Commons 'love those best, that most know and affect true liberty' (pp. 1-4).

10 *And . . . free*] Cf. 'the truth shall make you free' (John viii.

M.S.—I

32), and *P.L.* xii. 83–4 : after the Fall 'true Libertie / Is lost, which alwayes with right Reason dwells'.

Milton here identifies the 'voice of Truth' with 'freedom of speech', thus leading into the subject of licensing (l. 11). Cf. *Animadversions* : 'the voyce of Truth for these many yeares . . . hath not bin heard . . . [if now] long persecuted Truth, could not be suffer'd speak . . . twere hard, twere something pinching in a Kingdome of free spirits' (*C.M.* III i. 112) ; *Areopagitica* : 'to keep a narrow bridge of licencing where the challenger should passe . . . is but weaknes and cowardise in the wars of Truth' (iv. 348).

11 *Licence . . . libertie*] Cf. p. 32. I am not convinced by N. H. Henry's argument ('Who Meant Licence When They Cried Liberty ?', *M.L.N.* (1951), lxvi. 509–13) that Milton refers to the uneducated propagandists of divorce, whose freedom of movement from spouse to spouse brought his own more serious views into disrepute. There is no evidence that these people *railed* at Milton ; on the other hand, the *bawling* and *railing* of the Presbyterians against him, and their animal-nature, is a recurring topic in *Colasterion* : 'But if a man . . . must bee infested . . . with dorrs and horsflies . . . with bauling whippets, and shin-barkers, and these to bee set on by plot and consultation with a *Junto* of Clergy men and Licencers . . .' (*C.M.* iv. 271).

12 *For . . . good*] Cf. 'Liberty hath a sharp and double edge, fit only to be handled by Just and Vertuous Men' (*C.M.* xviii. 253) (Smart). The idea, which goes back to classical writers, was repeated several times by Milton, e.g. in *The Tenure of Kings and Magistrates* : 'none can love freedom heartilie, but good men ; the rest love not freedom, but licence' (*C.M.* v. 1).

13 *mark . . . roave*] To *rove* = to shoot with arrows at a mark selected at random and not of any fixed distance (*O.E.D.*). Milton means that his contemporaries shoot at the mark of liberty in a random, careless way, and miss the target completely, whereas he himself set to work systematically, according to the *known rules*, etc.

14 *For . . . blood*] The line seems to imply that the Civil War still continues. *For* = in spite of.

XII

TEXTS (i) Cambridge MS., rough draft (autograph) [MS. 1]; (ii) MS., fair copy (scribal) [MS. 2]; (iii) 1673.

TITLE (*Cf. p.* 113. *This sonnet was numbered* '12' *in MSS.* 1 + 2, *but became* 'XI' *in* 1673.)

COLLATION

1 A . . . writ] MS. 1 *etc.* (MS. 1 *orig.* I writt a book).

2 wov'n] MS. 1 *etc.* (MS. 1 *orig.* weav'd it).

3 The . . . walk'd] MS. 1 *etc.* (MS. 1 *orig.* It went off well about).

4 good . . . now] MS. 1 *etc.* (MS. 1 *orig.* good witts; but now is).

10 rugged] MS. 2, 1673; barbarous MS. 1 *altered to* rough hewn *altered to* rugged.

COMMENTARY

Publicly condemned for his *Doctrine and Discipline of Divorce* (cf. p. 198), Milton sought to reinforce his theory by citing scholarly opinions similar to his own, and by a more detailed examination of Scripture. In *Tetrachordon* he discussed the four decisive biblical passages (from the books of Genesis and Deuteronomy, from St. Matthew and the First Epistle to the Corinthians). His title will have caused some bewilderment, since it could not be understood without some acquaintance with Greek music — in which the tetrachords or scales consisted of four notes.

For the date cf. p. 117.

2 *And . . . stile*] i.e. meticulously devised, so that *matter, form and stile* all suited one another. It is unlikely that *form* = shape, since *Tetrachordon* is not a remarkably well-shaped treatise. Milton, I think, distinguishes *form* and *matter* as in Scholastic philosophy, where *form* = 'The essential determinant principle of a thing; that which makes anything (*matter*) a determinate species or kind of being' (*O.E.D.*, citing *Tetrachordon* ('the *Form* by which the thing is what it is'), *C.M.* iv. 101).

wov'n] Suggested, perhaps, by *Tetrachordon*, since *chord* could = string of a musical instrument.

3 *new*] Milton writes loosely, for his first divorce tract appeared a year and a half before *Tetrachordon*. Moreover, as he himself had stressed in the tracts, Martin Bucer, Sir John Cheke and others had discussed the *new subject* long before that, from a point of view similar to his own.

4 *Numbring*] measuring; including or comprising (a number of good intellects).

5-8 *Cries . . . Green*] Milton follows the epigrammatists, who also laughed at foolish readers at the book-stalls. Cf. Martial, *Epigrams*, XI. 1, and Jonson's *To my Booke-seller*:

> Nor haue my title-leafe on posts, or walls,
> Or in cleft-sticks, aduanced to make calls

> For termers, or some clarke-like seruing-man,
> Who scarse can spell th'hard names . . .
> (*Jonson* (1947), viii. 28)

Smart glossed *spelling fals* as 'interpreting amiss', comparing
sonnet XVII. 6, but Jonson's epigram suggests the more modern
sense.

Though the stall-readers of the day were used to finding
strange words on title-pages (e.g. Smectymnuus, Areopagitica,
Colasterion), there is a contemporary reference to the extravagance of 'Tetrachordon', in addition to sonnet XII. Milton, we
read in a squib, perhaps asked a friend to name one of his later
pamphlets 'that has a luckier hand at giving Titles to Books than
you have : For it is observ'd, you have always been very unfortunate that way. . . . As also in that other learned Labor of yours,
which you style *Tetrachordon*, that is to say, a Fiddle with four
strings ; but, as you render it, a Four-fold Cord, with which you
undertake . . . not to bind, but (most ridiculously) to unty
Matrimony' (*The Censure of the Rota*, by 'J. H.' (1660), p. 4).

7-8 *Mile-End Green*] So called because it lay about a mile from
the centre of old London. Masson says, 'it was a common in
Milton's time and the favourite terminus of a citizen's walk'
(Moody).

Classical poets split words as Milton does here, not necessarily
with a comical intention (e.g. Horace and Catullus). In *P.L.* x.
581, we find 'the wide- / Encroaching *Eve*'.

8 *Why*] This could be an adverb or an interjection.

8-9 *Gordon . . . Galasp*] 'The Civil War had made Englishmen
acquainted with many Scottish names, both of Cavaliers and
Covenanters, which seemed strange and harsh, and were made
more so by mispronunciation and misspelling. Those of Gordon
and Macdonald were brought into note by the campaigns of
Montrose, the Royalist army having officers who belonged to

both clans. Collcitto, i.e. *Coll Ciotach*, or "left-handed Colin",
was a familiar title given to one of the Macdonalds, who acted as
Montrose's lieutenant. Masson points out that the same chief
might also be called Gillespie; but there is no reason to believe
that Milton had heard of the circumstance, or had it in his mind
when he wrote the sonnet' (Smart).

9 *Galasp*] 'A Covenanter and member of the Assembly of
Divines, George Gillespie, was the most conspicuous bearer of
the name, which is much mutilated by the poet, and not by him
alone :—a certain "Mr Galaspy" preached before the House of
Commons in January 1657' (Smart).

George Gillespie died in December 1648, but he too appeared
in the *Journals* of the Commons, as 'Mr Gillaspie' (28 February
1643/4). And Newton observed long ago that in Bulstrode
Whitelocke's *Memorials* (1682) there is an entry in 1648 recording
the preaching of 'Mr *Galaspe*' (p. 306).

10-11 *Those . . . gasp*] 'In his treatise on Oratory, Quintilian
. . . discusses the choice of words for reasons of euphony, giving
the preference to such as are pleasant in sound, as well as immediately intelligible. . . . Uncouth proper names of foreign origin
were liable to objection because of their harshness of sound'
(Smart).

Milton's deleted word, '*barbarous* names', underlines the connection with Quintilian, to whose section on 'barbarisms' (I. 5 :
barbarismi) the sonnet refers. One such barbarism not mentioned
by Smart, but surely in Milton's mind, was 'adding a letter or
syllable to any word . . . *or taking one away*' (I. 5. 10) — hence
Galasp.

Quintilian repeatedly rebuked orators who proceed by fits and
starts, or pant, or have a halting delivery, and also disapproved of
'rigid and distended' eyes. To make Quintilian himself *stare and
gasp* helps to suggest that things have been turned topsy-turvy —

which is the complaint of the sonnet as a whole, in so far as Milton's contemporaries are more familiar with barbarisms than with Greek.

Cf. *Animadversions* : 'in dealing with an outlandish name they thought it best not to screw the English mouth to a harsh forreigne termination' (*C.M.* III i. 110).

10 *like . . . sleek*] '*like*, i.e. rugged like the names; *sleek*, smooth because familiar' (Verity). Cf. *P.R.* iv. 5 : The Tempter 'sleek't his tongue'.

12-14 *Thy . . . Greek*] Much debated. Smart showed that the introduction of the New Learning in King Edward's reign 'was accompanied by much prejudice and hostility'. Bishop Gardiner, the Chancellor of Cambridge University, opposed and finally stopped the teaching of the Erasmian pronunciation of Greek by Sir John Cheke, the university's first Professor of Greek, who in turn confessed in a Latin treatise of 1555 that 'the Greek language was hateful to many, and is so now; and there are those who dissuade young men from its study'.

Others, like J. Milton French, urge that for Milton Cheke's age was 'the purest and sincerest that ever shon yet on the reformation of this Iland' (*Tetrachordon*; *C.M.* iv. 231), so that 'it seems more likely that Milton, saturated as he was by Latin style, merely transposed the "like ours" from the spot where a modern writer might naturally put it. . . . He (or we) might probably have said in simpler prose, "Thy age hated not learning, like ours [i.e. as ours does], worse than toad or asp"' (*M.L.N.* (1955), lxx, 404–5).

I think that Smart is right. In the Preface to Cheke's *True Subiect to the Rebell* (1641), it was stressed that his age *hated learning* — there was 'an universall stupor & lethargy' — and Bishop Gardiner's repressive measures against Cheke were described (cf. H. Schultz in *M.L.N.* (1954), lxix, 495–7). Milton (in his *Tetrachordon*) and Cheke both 'taught Greek', and both experienced opposition from the 'barbarous'.

·XIII

TEXTS (i) Cambridge MS., rough draft (autograph) [MS. 1]; (ii) Cambridge MS., fair copy (autograph) [MS. 2]; (iii) Cambridge MS., scribal fair copy [MS. 3]; (iv) Henry Lawes, *Choice Psalms*, 1648 [1648]; (v) 1673.

TITLE (*For the various MS. titles cf. below*, p. 128.) To my Friend Mr. *Henry Lawes*. 1648; *To Mr*. H. Lawes, *on his Aires*. 1673.

COLLATION

3 Words . . . scan] words with just notes, wch till then us'd to scan MS. 1, *altered to* when most were wont to scan (*written twice and twice deleted. The third version was also written twice, and once deleted:*) words with just note & accent, not to scan MS. 1 *etc.*

4 committing] MS. 1, *altered to* misjoyning; committing MS. 2 *etc.*

5 worth] MS. 1, *altered to* wit (*deleted*); worth MS. 2 *etc.*

6 With . . . wan] and gives thee praise above the pipe of Pan MS. 1 (*partly deleted*); with praise anough for Envy to look wan MS. 2 *etc.* (anough MSS. 2 + 3; enough 1648, 1673).

7 after-age] MSS. 2 + 3; after age MS. 1 *etc.*

the] MSS. 2 + 3, 1648, 1673; a MS. 1.

8 That . . . tongue.] MSS. 2 + 3, 1648, 1673 (*orig.* aires MS. 2) ; that didst reform thy art, the cheif among MS. 1 ; . . . tongu 1673.

9 lend] MSS. 1–3, 1648 ; send 1673.

11 their] 1648, 1673 ; thir MSS. 1–2 ; theire MS. 3.

12-13 *Dante* . . . *sing*] *All texts*; MS. 1 *orig.* Fame by the Tuscan's leav, shall set thee higher / then old Casella whom Dante woo'd to sing (*Fletcher thinks that l. 13, which is badly blotted, first read:* then old Casell' whom Dante won to sing).

14 milder] *All texts*; MS. 1 *orig.* mildest.

COMMENTARY

Historians of music now think Milton's compliment to Lawes a little in excess of the facts. The new declamatory or recitative song, replacing the older madrigal as the first favourite of sophisticated audiences, was not *first taught* by Henry Lawes alone.

The declamatory and other forms of English song were the result of several forces at work during the first decades of the [seventeenth] century. They were not, as Milton states, the invention of one man, Henry Lawes. William Lawes, John Wilson, Simon Ives, Charles Coleman, John Gamble and many others were setting verse in precisely the same manner at precisely the same time. All were subject to new styles emanating from the humanistic revivals in France and Italy. . . .[1]

Campion also experimented with recitative, and challenged composers to couple the 'Words and the Notes lovingly together'. But, according to his biographer, Henry Lawes 'out-Campioned Campion by subordinating the notes to the words',[2] and thus

[1] Murray Lefkowitz, *William Lawes* (1960), p. 150. In his first draft Milton recognised that Lawes was not the sole inventor of the new music : 'that didst reform thy art, *the cheif among*' (l. 8).

[2] Willa M. Evans, *Henry Lawes* (1941), p. 29. Lawes himself explained : 'the way of *composition* I chiefly profess . . . is to shape *Notes* to the *Words* and

reversed the established rôles of music and poetry : whereas in the madrigal music came first in importance, in recitative the poetry determined the quality of the music.

This underlying shift in the relative importance of the text reflects the increasing stature of the poet in the artistic circles of the time . . . Lutenist, as well as madrigal, composers largely composed their own lyrics. . . . But with the increased interest on the part of literary men in Classical and Roman lyric forms during the Baroque, a gradual process of specialization set in. A generation of minor poets and dramatists, who were non-musicians, assiduously cultivated the now popular lyric style.[1]

Nearly all the leading poets of the age, and many minor ones, had verses set to music by Lawes ; not only *Aires* and *Hymn, or Story* but also masques and other entertainments. The *story* which gave him his greatest triumph as a composer was apparently Cartwright's *Ariadne Deserted* (cf. l. 11, note) ; Lawes's *Choice Psalms* followed the words of George Sandys ; he provided music for masques by Carew, Milton, Davenant, etc. ; and various poets expressed in verse their admiration of his genius, including Milton, Waller and Herrick.[2]

In the Cambridge Manuscript Milton headed his rough draft of the sonnet 'To my freind Mr Hen. Laws Feb. 9. 1645' (i.e. 1646). A scribe added a different heading to Milton's autograph fair copy, 'To Mr: Hen: Laws on the publishing of his Aires',

---

Sense' (ibid., p. 204). But in his verses to his friend John Wilson, published in the latter's *Psalterium Carolinum* (1657), Lawes acknowledged Wilson's leadership of the new school :

> Thou taught'st our Language, first, to speak in Tone.
> Gav'st the right accents and proportion ;
> And above all (to shew thy excellence)
> Thou understand'st good words, and do'st set sense ;
> Hadst none to imitate, and few will be
> Able t'express inimitably thee.
>   (Evans, p. 220).

[1] Lefkowitz, pp. 151–2.
[2] For the verses of Herrick and Waller, cf. Evans, pp. 54, 110 ; for a list of the poets whose works Lawes set to music, cf. Evans, pp. 239–40.

copied this exactly for the third (scribal) draft, but subsequently changed the third title to read 'To Mr: H. Lawes on his Aires', the form also found in the Milton edition of 1673. It is a reasonable guess that already on 9 February 1645/6, an edition of Lawes's *Airs* was projected — but not that it was abandoned because of the 'crushing news of the death of his brother'.[1]

Christened 5 January 1595/6, Lawes was fifty years old in 1646. (Milton wrote his sonnet to a man thirteen years his senior, but gives an impression of complete equality.) As a composer he had long been celebrated — and this accounts for the prominence of his name on the title-page of Milton's *Poems*, issued 2 January 1645/6: 'The Songs were set in Musick by Mr. Henry Lawes Gentleman of the Kings Chappel, and one of His Maiesties Private Musick'. The publisher, Humphrey Moseley, who put the same blurb on Waller's poems in 1645, clearly thought that Lawes's name would help to sell the book, though the Civil War was still dragging on and Lawes was a noted Royalist. That Milton, strongly committed to the Parliamentary party, should be prepared at such a time to write warmly of Lawes,[2] and later to sanction the inclusion of the poem in a book loyally dedicated to the imprisoned king, becomes less surprising when one recollects, in addition to the composer's fame, the special relationship of Milton and Lawes over a period of years.

Masson conjectured long ago that the two may well have met

[1] Cf. Evans, p. 168, who dated William Lawes's death 'some four or five days after Milton had written the first draft of this sonnet'. William Lawes died in September 1645 (Lefkowitz, pp. 20–1). W. R. Parker thought that the sonnet's scribal headings were added as late as 1653, when Henry Lawes's *Ayres and Dialogues* began to appear (*P.Q.* (1949), xxviii. 159, note), but since (i) Milton's sonnet was not printed by Lawes in 1653, and (ii) was already printed in Henry and William Lawes's *Choice Psalms* (1648), it is more likely that a volume of *Airs* was planned before 1648. A cancelled reading of Milton's second draft ('That with smooth *aires* . . .') gives some support to this, the older view.

[2] Milton's feelings are revealed by the difference between his title's formal 'Mr Hen. Laws', and his more intimate opening, 'Harry, . . .'; and also by the change of 'old Casella' to 'his Casella', since Dante's relationship to Casella parallels Milton's to Lawes.

during the poet's boyhood at the house of his father, a well-known musician in London.[1] It is also a conjecture, but a highly plausible one, that Lawes and Milton collaborated on *Arcades*: Lawes taught music in the Bridgewater family, by whom this entertainment was produced at Harefield, and the part of 'the Genius of the Wood' seems designed for him, as that of 'the Attendant Spirit' in *Comus* certainly was a little thereafter. (Neither the date of *Arcades*, nor the date of Lawes's commencement as music-teacher with the Bridgewaters, is known.) Milton's biographers therefore assume that the poet and musician were on familiar terms before 1634, the year of *Comus*: and some also believe that in this major work Lawes not only played a leading rôle, and composed the music for the songs, but even advised his younger colleague in the actual writing, drawing on his professional experience as both musician and actor. Three years later Lawes took the initiative in publishing *Comus*, apparently with Milton's consent.[2] In the following year (1638) Lawes secured for Milton a warrant to leave the king's dominions, thus making possible the famous continental journey: his letter to Milton enclosing the warrant still survives.[3] Subsequent recorded points of contact include the publication of Milton's *Poems*, the writing of Milton's sonnet (both 1646), the publication of *Choice Psalms* (1648), and the publication in *Ayres and Dialogues* (1653) of complimentary verses by Milton's nephews Edward and John Phillips. Lawes died in 1662.

2, 8   *our*] Milton seems to have been aware that by European standards Lawes was not quite so original.

span] measure ; harness, yoke.

3   *accent*] i.e. musical accent, the marks placed over words to show the various notes or tunes or phrases to which they were sung (*O.E.D.*).

[1] *Poetical Works*, i. 149.   [2] Masson, op. cit., i. 171.   [3] Evans, pp. 148–52.

4 Midas *Ears*] Midas, King of Phrygia, preferred the music of Pan's reeds to that of Apollo's lyre. To punish him Apollo turned his ears into those of an ass (Ovid, *Metamorphoses*, xi. 146 ff.).

committing] combining.

5 *exempts*] singles out, selects. From Horace, *Odes*, i. i. 32 — 'Secernunt populo' (Richardson).

6 *Envy . . . wan*] Milton adapts the phrase 'pale with envy' (cf. *Henry V*, v. ii. 341).

7 *thou . . . writ*] From Horace, *Odes*, i. vi. 1 — '*Scriberis* Vario fortis et hostium / victor' (Newton).

8 *aire*] melody, music.

humor] comply with the peculiar nature of; indulge. Citing Walton, *Compleat Angler* (1653), *O.E.D.* gives another sense that would fit the context: to give a particular character or style to ('This Song was well humor'd by the maker . . .').

9-11 *Thou . . . Story*] It must have been a common conceit that Poetry can repay the debt it owes to related arts. Cf. Jonson's lines to Edward Alleyn, the actor: ''Tis iust, that who did giue / So many *Poets* life, by one should liue' (*Jonson*, viii. 57). But it was probably more usual to imagine Music lending its wings to Verse than the other way round; cf. Edward Phillips' lines to Lawes (influenced by Milton's sonnet ?) —

> Thy Lay's that wont to lend a soaring wing,
> And to my tardy Muse fresh ardour bring.
>
> (Evans, p. 212)

10 Phoebus] Cf. l. 4, note. In his famous sonnet, 'If music and sweet poetry agree, As they needs must, the sister and the brother', Barnfield stressed the close relationship of music and poetry, and mentioned that 'one god is god of both'. Milton no doubt refers to Apollo at this point for the same reason.

11 *Story*] Explained with a marginal note in *Choice Psalms* —
'The story of Ariadne set by him in Music' (i.e. Cartwright's
poem, *The Complaint of Ariadne*).   Several editors have called
this 'the only annotation we have by Milton himself'.[1]   There
are others, of course, in a few of the prose works, but this is the
only one accompanying a poem by Milton.   That it was written
'by Milton himself' seems doubtful, however, since it appears
neither in the MS. nor in 1673.

12-14 Dante . . . *Purgatory*] 'The reference is to the passage
in Dante's *Purgatorio*, Cant. II., where he represents himself as
meeting, in a crowd of other souls, the musician Casella, who
had been his dear friend in life, and asking him to sing, even
there, if it were permissible, one of those love-songs in which
he excelled on earth.   Casella complies, and sings a song of
Dante's own' (Masson).

'Dante addresses him as *Casella mio*' (Smart).

Lawes having set to music some of Milton's poetry, the relationship of Dante and Casella was evidently intended to mirror
that of Milton and his friend.   In choosing the Italians for this
purpose Milton may have been influenced by the fact that they
belonged, at the time of their reunion, to different worlds, the
living and the dead, just as Milton and Lawes belonged to different
sides during the Civil War.   The precise date with which Milton
headed the sonnet (9 February 1645/6), coming shortly before
the end of the First Civil War, may indeed commemorate the
first meeting of the two friends after a separation of years.

14 *milder shades*] 'shades comparatively much less horrible than
those which Dante describes in the *Inferno*' (Warton). As Milton
first wrote *mildest*, and changed this to *milder*, J. S. Diekhoff has
urged that he 'is not thinking of the region in which Dante met
Casella as milder with reference to the *Inferno*, but, remembering

[1] E.g. H. F. Fletcher in *Poetical Works*, i. 368.

his Dante, speaks of the shores of Purgatory, where the meeting takes place, first as the "mildest" part of Purgatory itself and then as "milder" than other regions of Purgatory' (*M.L.N.* (1937), lii. 409–10).

XIV

TEXTS (i) Cambridge MS., rough draft (autograph) [MS. 1]; (ii) Cambridge MS., copy (autograph) [MS. 2]; (iii) Cambridge MS., fair copy (scribal) [MS. 3]; (iv) 1673.

TITLE On ye religious memorie of Mrs Catharine Thomason my christian freind deceas'd [16 *deleted*] Decem. 1646 MS. 1 (*deleted title.* 'Thomason' *was first written* 'Thomasin'. *The* '16' *before* 'Decem.' *suggests that Milton meant to write* '1646' *but changed his mind and added the month.*)

COLLATION

The first draft reads as follows (omitting revisions):

> When Faith & Love, that parted from thee never,
>> Had rip'n'd thy just soul to dwell with God,
>> Meekly thou didst resigne this earthy clod
> Of Flesh & sin, wch man from heav'n doth sever.
> Thy Works, & Almes, and all thy good Endeavor
>> Strait follow'd thee the path that Saints have trod
>> Still as they journey'd from this dark abode
> Up to ye Realm of peace & Joy for ever,
> Faith who led on ye way, & knew them best
>> thy handmaids, clad them o're with purple beames
>> and azure wings, thence up they flew so drest
> And spake the truth of thee in glorious theames
>> before the Judge, who thenceforth bidd thee rest,
>> and drink thy fill of pure immortal streames

1 which] MS. 2 *etc.*; that MS. 1.

3 load] MS. 1 (*altered from* clod), *etc.*

4 Of . . . sever] MS. 1 (*altered from first draft*), *etc.*

from Life] from blis MS. 3 *orig.*

6-8 Staid . . . ever] MS. 1 (*altered from first draft, above*), *etc.*

9 Love . . . best] *Milton corrected* MS. 1 *to read* Faith shew'd
yᵉ way, & shee who saw them best *copied this line in* MS. 2,
then changed to final version in MS. 2.

11 that] MS. 1 (*altered from* thence), *etc.*

12 spake] MSS. 1–3 ; speak 1673.

in] MSS. 1–2 ; on MS. 3, 1673.

COMMENTARY

We owe the identification of Mrs Thomason, and our knowledge
of her life and character, to Smart, who first showed that her
name was not Mrs 'Thomson', as previous editors mistakenly
read it in the Cambridge Manuscript. She turns out to have
been the wife of George Thomason, the bookseller who col-
lected the famous Thomason Tracts, the 22,000 books and
pamphlets of the Civil War period now housed in the British
Museum.

Thomason's wife was born Katharine Hutton. At an early
age she was left, by her father's death, to the guardianship of her
uncle, Henry Fetherstone, the bookseller, with whom Thomason
served his apprenticeship. Married around 1631, she had nine
children, and died in December 1646, being buried in St. Dunstan's in the West, Fleet Street, on 12 December.

It appears from her husband's will (proved in 1666) that Mrs
Thomason owned an extensive library. Her knowledge, thought
Smart, 'must have been wide, amounting to erudition'. Her
husband referred to her several times in the will as his 'late dear
and only wife', 'my late dear wife' etc., and we may glimpse

her character in the funeral sermon for her daughter Elizabeth, preached in 1659 by Edward Reynolds:

She was both in bodily resemblance, and in moral imitation the transcript of a gracious mother. . . . She was of a lowly minde, and in special beautified with that grace which the Apostle calleth the *ornament of a meek and quiet spirit.* . . . She lived for the space of an year in my family, with so much sweetnesse and innocency of conversation, that I believe never any could observe in all that time the least appearance of any passion in her (p. 64).

Milton seems to have been friendly with both the Thomasons. Copies of his books inscribed 'ex dono authoris' survive in the Thomason Tracts; and it is generally agreed that the bookseller mentioned in Milton's letter to Carlo Dati, 1647, as his intimate friend, *mihi familiarissimo*, was George Thomason.

Though the references to Mrs Thomason's *Alms* are a commonplace of the epitaph-genre (cf. p. 46), it is worth observing that her husband must have been a man of exceptional means. How many of the Tracts were given to him, rather than purchased, is not now ascertainable: yet this was by no means the only magnificently conceived Thomason collection. His wife's private library was clearly a substantial one. And after her death he travelled in Italy, in 1647, and, on his return, printed a catalogue 'of Books, in the Eastern Languages, of very great Value, late brought out of *Italy*, and having been the Library of a learned *Rabbi* there' — for which Parliament paid him £500.[1] At the time of his death Thomason was however described as 'a poore man' (Henry R. Plomer, *A Dictionary of Booksellers and Printers* (1641–67), 1907).

1 *Faith . . . Love*] Cf. *Christian Doctrine*, chap. I: 'Christian doctrine is comprehended under two divisions: Faith, or the

[1] *Journals of the House of Commons*, v. 512, where the name is spelt *Thomason*. On p. 617 it is *Thomasine*. Milton changed *Thomasin* to *Thomason* in the MS.: evidently both forms were in use.

M.S.——K

knowledge of God; and Love, or the worship of God' (*C.M.* xiv. 23); *A Treatise of Civil Power*: 'What evangelic religion is, is told in two words, faith and charitie; or beleef and practise' (*C.M.* vi. 21). The Epistles of Paul, of which we are also reminded when *Faith* and *Works* are discussed, frequently stress *Faith* and *Love*: 1 Cor. xiii. 13, Eph. i. 15, Col. i. 4, 1 Thess. i. 3.

2 *ripen'd*] Cf. p. 68.

dwell . . . God] Cf. Ps. cxl. 13 : 'the upright shall dwell in thy presence'.

4 *Death . . . Life*] A popular paradox. Cf. John xii. 25 : 'he that hateth his life in this world shall keep it unto life eternal'.

5 *Thy . . . Endeavour*] Cf. 'Thy prayers and thine alms are come up for a memorial before God', Acts x. 4; 'Blessed are the dead which die in the Lord . . . their works do follow them' (Rev. xiv. 13) (Keightley).

Milton here seems to glance at the theological debate about justification. Are we justified by Faith, or by Faith and Works ? In the *Christian Doctrine*, citing Rom. iii. 24–8, Gal. ii. 16, Jas. ii. 24, he ruled that 'Faith has its own works, which may be different from the works of the law' (*C.M.* xvi. 37–9).

7 *golden rod*] The staff of office of Athene in Homer, *Od.* xvi. 172, is transferred to Faith. Somnus has the *golden rod* in the Latin poets, who were copied by Drummond (Pattison). Warton and Verity suggest a connection with the 'golden reed' held by the angel in Rev. xxi. 15 — a likely source, since there is a cross-reference to 'a reed like unto a *rod*' (Rev. xi. 1).

8 *Follow'd . . . up*] In his *Christian Doctrine*, parts of which were composed in the 1640's, Milton denied 'that the soul is exempt from death, and that when divested of the body, it wings its way, or is conducted by angels, directly to its appointed place of reward or punishment' (i. 13 ; *C.M.* xv. 237). In short, he

believed in the Mortalist Heresy, according to which the soul dies
with the body and remains dead till the Resurrection. (Cf.
Masson, *Life*, vi. 832–3 ; *P.L.* x. 782 ff.) If he already shared
these unorthodox opinions in 1646 he decided to ignore them in
this 'traditional' sonnet — just as he preferred not to obtrude his
Arianism in *Paradise Lost*.

10–11 *clad . . . wings*] Todd compared Phineas Fletcher, *Upon
the B. of Exon. Doct. Hall his Meditations*:

> Most blessèd soul, that, lifted up with *wings*
> *Of faith and love*, leaves this base habitation ;
> And, scorning sluggish earth, *to heav'n up springs*.

Cf. T. Valentine, *Christs Counsell* (1647), p. 16 : In heaven the
saints shall wear no apparel, 'yet that *stola corporis* shall be glorious, as that the beames thereof shall be much better then any
garment to cover them' ; *The Virgin-Martyr* (*Massinger*, ed. F.
Cunningham (1897), p. 13) : 'Fight well, and thou shalt see, after
these wars, / Thy head wear sunbeams, and thy feet touch stars'.

10 *purple*] Could mean 'bright-hued, brilliant'.

12 *Theams*] strains. Grierson argued for this musical sense
since 'the use of "theme" for the plainsong or *canto fermo* of a
contrapuntal piece goes back to the sixteenth century' (*T.L.S.*
(15 January 1925), p. 40).

14 *And . . . streams*] 'The allusion is to the waters of life, and
more particularly to Ps. xxxvi. 8, 9 — "Thou shalt make them
drink of the river of thy pleasures. For with thee is the fountain
of life"' (Warton). Cf. 'And he shewed me a pure river of
water of life, clear as crystal, proceeding out of the throne of God
and of the Lamb' ; 'And whosoever will, let him take the water
of life freely' (Rev. xxii. 1, 17) (Smart).

XV

TEXTS (i) Cambridge MS., autograph [MS.]; (ii) Edward
Phillips, 1694 [1694].

TITLE On yᵉ Lord Gen. Fairfax at yᵉ seige of Colchester MS.
(*deleted title*); To my Lord FAIRFAX. 1694.

COLLATION

2   Filling each mouth] MS.; And fills all Mouths 1694.

4   that] MS.; which 1694.

5   vertue] MS.; Valour 1694.

6   though] MS.; while 1694.

8   their] MS.; her 1694.[1]

10   can Warr] MS., 1694.[1]

endless warr] MS.; Acts of War 1694.

11   Truth, and Right] MS.; injur'd Truth 1694.

12   cleard from the shamefull] MS.; be rescu'd from the 1694.

14   share] MS.; shares 1694.

COMMENTARY

Sir Thomas Fairfax (1612–71) campaigned energetically against
the Royalists in the North in the early phases of the Civil War,

---

[1] J. T. Shawcross (*N. & Q.* (1955), cc. 195–6) has argued that in the MS.
'their' (l. 8) originally read 'her', and was tampered with by a later hand, and
that 'Warr' (l. 10) should be read 'Warrs'. Concerning *their* he noted that
(i) Milton never used this spelling in MS.; (ii) 'her' is the form in 1694; (iii)
'her' disposes of the problem of the winged Hydra (cf. l. 7, note).

and distinguished himself at Marston Moor (1644). Appointed
commander-in-chief of the New Model Army with the support
of Cromwell, his senior by thirteen years, he justified the confidence placed in him by winning the Battle of Naseby (1645). He
seems to have been a commander of great personal courage,
though some have questioned his generalship, ascribing his victories partly or largely to his able lieutenants, Cromwell in
particular. When the struggle between Presbyterians and Independents came to a head *c.* 1646–8 (cf. p. 37), Fairfax was
forced to take sides — and, despite his Presbyterian sympathies,
threw in his lot with the Army and therefore with Independency.
The Army, after publishing in Fairfax's name various petitions, declarations, resolutions, remonstrances, etc., condemning
its Presbyterian antagonists, at last marched on London (1647),
and for a time took over control of the government.

Presbyterian Scotland now thought that the king, though held
prisoner on the Isle of Wight, would be the best ally for its
purposes, and signed its secret treaty with him. On 8 July 1648,
the *false North* (i.e. the Scots) invaded England once more in the
name of the Covenant, the English Royalists having broken out
in *new rebellions* elsewhere — in the Fleet, in Yorkshire, in Wales
and in the counties around London. Fairfax (*Lord* Fairfax since
his father's death in March 1648, though already *Lord General* as
commander-in-chief) subdued the revolters in the London area,
his siege of Colchester (June–28 August), and Cromwell's defeat
of the Scots at Preston (August), effectually terminating the war.
Despite these set-backs to their cause the English Presbyterians,
regaining their ascendancy in Parliament, continued to disregard
the wishes of the Army : like the Scots they tried to come to an
understanding with the king, hoping to put down the Independents
with his help. Petitions now began to reach Fairfax from the
towns and shires, and from his own regiments, calling for justice
against offenders, repudiating Parliament as a mere faction, and

suggesting a General Council of the Army to consider large-scale reforms (Autumn 1648). Such a general Council was held, and published its *Grand Army Remonstrance*, or ultimatum to Parliament, in November. The Army then once more marched on London, determined to bring the king to trial. Excluding members of the Commons hostile to its plans (Pride's Purge, 6 December), it prevailed upon the House to vote for the trial, which was followed at once by the king's execution.

From subsequent events it grows clear that in the autumn of 1648 the Army 'strategists' pushed on Fairfax, forcing him to go further than he wished. Though one of the commissioners for the king's trial, he only attended one meeting and then shrank from accepting responsibility. He remained commander-in-chief of the Parliamentary forces, but refused on conscientious grounds to lead the army into Scotland against Charles II in 1650, and resigned. Thereafter he lived in retirement and interfered in public affairs scarcely at all. Yet, whether or not Fairfax was pushed, the public attitude to him after the siege of Colchester throws some light on Milton's sonnet. Smart wrote —

The reorganisation of the State by the victor of Naseby, which Milton at one time hoped for, was never accomplished, nor even begun.

The many petitioners who addressed him desired Fairfax and the Army to oppose the encroachments of a Presbyterian Parliament. This, rather than a full-scale reorganisation of the State, was also Milton's wish, and Fairfax did what was expected.

After 1648 Milton alluded to Fairfax in other writings. Only a few months after composing the sonnet he condemned Fairfax's backwardness at the king's trial, with considerable heat.[1] The more considered judgment of the *Second Defence* (1654) is better known :

Nor must I forget you, Fairfax, in whom nature and the divine favour have conspired to unite the greatest modesty, the most exemplary sanctity of life, with the highest courage. . . .[2]

[1] Cf. Masson, *Life*, iv. 70.   [2] *C.M.* viii. 217.

3 *jealous*] The secondary meanings 'suspiciously vigilant' and 'fearful' are perhaps present.

4 *daunt remotest kings*] 'Who dreaded the example of England, that their monarchies would be turned into republics' (Warton).

5 *unshak'n*] A trisyllable, despite Milton's apostrophe. Cf. *brok'n*, l. 8, *wov'n* (XII. 2), *reck'ns* (XVII. 12), etc.

vertue] 'Here *virtue* is used in the Latin sense as *valour*' (Smart). But Milton surely compliments moral virtue as well — a favourite topic in the sonnets (cf. IX, X, XIV, XX). J. H. Finlay compared Horace's vision of civic virtue stamping out the Hydra of rebellion (*Odes*, IV, iv. 61–2), and similar Horatian odes (*Harvard Studies in Classical Philology* (1937), xlviii. 41, 59).

7 *Hydra heads*] One of the labours of Hercules was to kill the Hydra, a nine-headed monster. Hercules found that as soon as he crushed one head two others appeared in its place. Warton thought that the Hydra's *wings* may have been suggested by 'a controverted word' in the *Ion* of Euripides. (The *wings* of an army may also have suggested the image.)

8 *brok'n league*] The Solemn League and Covenant of 1643 was, according to the English Puritans, broken by the Scots when they marched into England in July 1648, to aid Charles I.

to . . . wings] 'To imp was a term in falconry, which has furnished many metaphors to English poets. If a falcon had some feathers in its wing broken, its flight became weaker and less sure; and to remedy the loss new feathers were inserted, the new being fastened with fine wire to the stumps of the old, — a process known as imping' (Smart).

11 *Truth*] Milton and other Independents had good reason to fear that *Truth* would suffer *Violence*. As recently as May, 1648, the Presbyterians in Parliament had passed a new law making it a capital offence to persist in heretical errors (Masson, *Life*, iii. 600–1). Milton naturally identified himself with *Truth*, and he and his beliefs were now seriously threatened. Compare also XI. 10, XVI. 4 and *New Forcers* 9–12.

12 *Public Faith*] Not in *O.E.D.*; scarcely discussed by Milton's editors.[1] The meanings of the phrase will appear from the following quotations. (i) 'The Publique Faith engaged to such as will advance Money, Horse, Arms, &c.' — Parliament ordered that all loans 'shall be repaid with Interest out of the Publique Stock of the Kingdome; for which they do engage the Publique Faith' (Scobell, *A Collection of Acts and Ordinances* (1658), p. 40: April 1643). (ii) In 1651 the Commons set up a committee 'to take into Consideration the Business of the publick Faith; and to prepare a Draught of a Commission to be sent into the several Counties, for ascertaining the publick Faith; and to bring in ... Qualifications of the publick Faith fit to be satisfied' (*Journals of the House of Commons*, vii. 79).

Initially *public faith* meant simply 'national honour'. But in Milton's day the phrase was widely used to refer to a form of National Debt incurred by the Parliament: placed beside *Public Fraud, Avarice and Rapine*, this is clearly its significance in the sonnet. There was, in fact, a general impatience in the 1640's concerning 'that empty bag called by fooles *fides publica*, by wise men *fides punica*',[2] both in the Army, whose very considerable arrears were promised again and again 'on the public faith', and among the Parliament's private creditors — of whom Milton seems to have been a typical example of disappointment.

It is reported . . . that Mr. Milton had lent most of his Personal Estate upon the Publick Faith; which when he somewhat earnestly

---

[1] Warburton glossed '*publick faith*, the security given by the parliament to the City-contributions for carrying on the war'.

[2] *The Mysterie of the Two Iunto's, Presbyterian and Independent* (1647), p. 3 (by 'Theoph. Verax').

and warmly pressed to have restored . . . after a long and chargeable
Attendance, met with very sharp Rebukes. . . . And he had not
probably mended his worldly condition in those days, but by per-
forming such Service for them, as afterwards he did, for which scarce
anything would appear too great.[1]

As Milton's 'service' began in 1649 it is likely that his 'long
and chargeable Attendance' overlapped with the writing of his
sonnet in 1648, or at least that the 'very sharp Rebukes' terminating his suit came not long before: the anger of his last lines
therefore reflects not only the woeful state of England but also
a highly personal sense of wrong.

There may be another personal connection with the Public
Faith — but I am sceptical about it. It has been noticed that
'John Milton' was named with several others in an ordinance
of Parliament of 24 April 1648, as a commissioner to collect 'the
Arreares of the Assessments for the Army' in 'Tower ward'.
J. Milton French commented:

It is not likely that this reference applies to the poet, who lived too far
from the Tower to be chosen for such work. But there is nothing
impossible about it. . . .[2]

A 'Major John Milton' known from other records,[3] who lived
in St. Dunstan's-in-the-East in Tower St. Ward, is, I think, the
obvious man with whom to identify the commissioner. Nevertheless the ordinance serves to remind us that Fairfax's army
suffered from the *Avarice* of such citizens as refused to pay their
assessments and would sympathise with Milton's *cri de cœur*.

13 *Public Fraud*] 'By the year 1648 it had become a charge
of the Independents and Army-chiefs against the less resolute
Parliamentarians that they had mismanaged and misappropriated
the public revenues, and that their half-hearted policy against
Charles arose from a dread of being called to account' (Masson).

---

[1] *Mr John Miltons Character of the Long Parliament* (1681), 'To the Reader'.
[2] *Life Records*, ii. 218. [3] Cf. Masson, *Life*, ii. 484.

In particular the Army resented the fact that the Presbyterian Parliament, anxious to rid itself of Army Independents, had paid arrears to soldiers who disbanded but had been less generous to those who remained in service.

XVI

TEXTS (i) Cambridge MS., scribal copy [MS.]; (ii) Edward Phillips, 1694 [1694].

TITLE To the Lord Generall Cromwell May 1652 On the proposalls of certaine ministers at ye Commtee for Propagation of the Gospell MS. *deleted*; TO Oliver Cromwell. 1694.

COLLATION

1 who . . . cloud] MS.; that . . . Croud 1694.

2 detractions] MS.; distractions 1694.

5 And . . . proud] MS.; *omitted* 1694.

6 Hast . . . pursu'd] MS.; And Fought God's Battels, and his Work pursu'd, 1694.

7 *Darwen* stream] MS.; *Darwent* Streams 1694.

8 resounds] MS.; resound 1694.

9 And . . . wreath] MS. (*orig.* And twentie battles more), 1694. (*The scribe erroneously deleted* Dunbarr feild, l. 8, *and wrote above it* Worsters laureat wreath.)

11 No . . . warr] MS.; No less than those of War 1694. arise] aries MS.

12 with] MS.; in 1694.

COMMENTARY

On 10 February 1652 a petition to Parliament brought by a
group of Independent ministers occasioned the questioning of
Milton, in his capacity as government licenser, and, indirectly,
the famous sonnet to Cromwell. John Owen, Cromwell's chap-
lain in Ireland and Scotland and later Vice-Chancellor of Oxford,
together with Bridge, Goodwin, Nye and Simpson and others
anxious to set up an Established Church (cf. p. 38), submitted
various documents on this subject to Parliament and also a copy
of the Racovian Catechism, a Socinian pamphlet lately printed
in England which they wished to get banned. The Commons
at once nominated a committee of forty to examine the petition,
and a committee of fourteen to confer with the ministers and
'to consider with them upon such proposals as shall be offered
for the Better Propagation of the Gospel'.[1] To this smaller
committee all interested parties despatched their views on
Church establishment for months on end : Milton's sonnet to
Cromwell, one of the forty and one of the fourteen, was far from
being the only attempt to influence opinion at this time. The
most important suggestions came from the Independent ministers
themselves, who produced their *Humble Proposals*, fifteen in
number and widely publicised in print, to define the limits of
toleration. These proposals seriously restricted the freedom of
worship of dissenters, whose preachers, it was urged, should pro-
cure a testimonial from two or more State ministers, failing which
they were to be suppressed. As in the 1640's, Milton denounced
the attempt *to bind our soules with secular chaines*; he must have
been the more disappointed in that history was repeating itself :
the *new foes* were his former allies (cf. p. 37).

Fortunately, as Milton would think, the Tolerationists had
highly placed friends. Of these the most forceful was Cromwell
— who, Smart reminds us, had already declared 'that he had

---

[1] Cf. Masson, *Life*, iv. 390.

rather that Mahometanism were permitted among us than that one of God's children should be persecuted'. Sir Henry Vane the younger felt as charitably towards the very Socinians, and Milton complimented him on his understanding of the boundaries of spiritual and civil authority,[1] in effect the same subject as that of the present sonnet.

Milton took an interest in the Committee for Propagation of the Gospel because he always resisted intolerance on principle — and also because he was himself examined at the committee's instigation. For the Socinians' *Racovian Catechism* deposited in Parliament by John Owen and his friends was actually licensed by Milton, whose name was mentioned in Parliament on 2 April 1652, when some of the blasphemies of the catechism were detailed: denial of the Trinity, denial of the divinity of Christ, denial of the doctrine of Original Sin, and so on. Parliament ruled that the book was 'blasphemous, erroneous and scandalous', and ordered that all copies should be publicly burned. Milton's friend Leo de Aitzema, agent of the Hanse towns in London, recorded current rumours and, apparently, Milton's defence, as early as 5 March:

There was recently printed here the Socinian *Racovian Catechism*. This was frowned upon by the Parliament; the printer says that Mr. Milton had licensed it; Milton, when asked, said Yes, and that he had published a tract on that subject, that men should refrain from forbidding books; that in approving of that book he had done no more than what his opinion was.[2]

The implications of Milton's appeal to Cromwell have never been fully explained by his editors, who overlooked his use of a once-popular catch-phrase. Throughout the 1640's and 1650's supporters of the Parliamentary party signed themselves in a multitude of pamphlets 'by a lover of *peace and truth* (or, of truth

---

[1] In sonnet XVII. For Vane and the Socinians cf. John Willcock's *Life of Sir Henry Vane the Younger* (1913), p. 229.   [2] *Life Records*, iii. 206.

and peace)', a phrase as much repeated in its day as 'the good old cause' and '*salus populi suprema lex*'. Some did so in allusion to the Solemn League and Covenant (1643), the concluding words of which summarised its aim as the establishing of truth (i.e. 'true' religion) and peace;[1] others, no doubt, without any such precise intention. Milton, a precisian where words were concerned, must have known of these associations, for he had signed the Covenant, which was in any case read publicly in every congregation on every fast day. Reminding Cromwell of the ideals of the Covenant, which looked forward to religious uniformity in Scotland and England, Milton proceeds in the sonnet to list some of the bloody consequences, the battles of Preston (1648), Dunbar (1650) and Worcester (1651). It is surely no accident that he cites three of Cromwell's victories against the Scots Presbyterians rather than his triumphs over English royalists or Irish rebels.[2] Through the Covenant with the Parliamentary faction the Scots had hoped to extend their brand of Presbyterianism into England, then, disappointed in this alliance, made their secret treaty with Charles I for the same purpose

[1] The Covenant ended with the promise that signatories will 'endeavour . . . to amend our lives, and each one to go before another in the example of a real reformation, that the Lord may turn away His wrath and heavy indignation, and establish these Churches and kingdoms in truth and peace. . . .' Cf. W. Goode, *The Discoverie of a Publique Spirit* (1645), after a reference to the Covenant: 'and now it must be your care . . . that wee may have such a hedge about the Vineyard, as will preserve *Truth* and *Peace*' (p. 32); the *Declaration* of the Scottish Parliament, 21 July 1648: 'being engaged by the joynt Declaration of both Kingdoms never to lay down Arms till Truth and Peace be setled in this Island' (p. 17); *The Groans of Kent* (1648) ends with the wish that the Army may compose 'the unhappy differences of the Nation upon the pillars of peace and truth' (Thomason Tracts, E. 453 (4)); *Englands Sole Remedy . . . By a Lover of Peace and Truth* (1648) (Thomason Tracts, E. 453 (7)); *To all that love Peace and Truth. The Declaration of the well-affected Non-Subscribers* (1648) (Thomason Tracts, E. 453 (17)). There are many other similar allusions in the pamphlets of the period. Cf. also pp. 31, 150.

[2] At Preston and Dunbar the Scots fought against Cromwell more or less unaided; at Worcester about 2,000 English royalists supported 10,000 Scots (*Boscobel* (1660), p. 7), but Parliament and the writers of the time referred to this as a victory against the Scots.

in 1647 (cf. p. 37), and later forced Charles II to take the Covenant, in 1650 — events which led directly to *Darwen stream, Dunbarr feild* and *Worster*. Cromwell himself had warned the Scots against their attempts to impose uniformity of religion, and against using the Covenant as a cover for less than respectable political manœuvring.

Is it therefore infallibly agreeable to the Word of God, all that *you* say ? I beseech you, in the bowels of Christ, think it possible you may be mistaken. . . . There may be . . . a carnal confidence upon misunderstood and misapplied precepts, which may be called spiritual drunkenness. There may be a *Covenant* made with Death and Hell ![1]

Milton had come to see the 'ridling Covenant' as a danger to genuine 'peace and truth' by 1649 already, and inveighed against the Scots as 'misobservers of the Covnant'.[2] His friend Marchamont Needham, in his semi-official *The Case of the Commonwealth of England*, 1650, wrote a chapter 'Concerning the Scots' exposing their abuses of the Covenant, opening with sentiments worthy of Dr. Johnson.

I am sorry I must waste Paper upon this Nation ; but seeing They make Themselves Considerable by being troublesome, it will not be amisse to sound the Depth of their present Design. . . .

Milton's sonnet to Cromwell expressed the more inflamed feelings of the English in the spring of 1652 — to which Sir Thomas Urquhart, a Scots prisoner in London, also testified, regretfully, in the March of that year :

[there is] nothing in the mouthes almost of all this country more common then the words of the *perfidious Scot*, the *treacherous Scot*, the *false brother*, the *covetous Scot*, and *knot of knaves*, and other suchlike indignities fixed upon the whole Nation. . . .[3]

It is against this background of recent invasions from the north that we must judge Milton's approval of a general who had

[1] Cf. Masson, *Life*, iv. 197.
[2] *The Tenure of Kings and Magistrates* and *Eikonoklastes* (*C.M.* v. 36, 162).
[3] *Ekskubalauron* (1652), A7.

ploughed his *glorious way*, to all intents, through the *blood of Scotts*.[1]

As is well-known, Milton's attitude to Cromwell in the sonnet compares interestingly with his admonition to the Protector in the *Second Defence* of 1654. Despite the dissolution of the Rump Parliament in 1653, which transformed many distinguished republicans, such as Bradshaw and Vane, into critics or enemies of Cromwell, Milton still applauded his 'extraordinary and almost supernatural virtue'. Yet he no longer regarded Cromwell as a fellow-Tolerationist, a believer in Absolute Voluntaryism in matters spiritual, for the Protector had at last made manifest his sympathy with John Owen and the Independents, and was publishing ordinances to halt the move towards Church-Disestablishment. Masson, in fact, suggested that those who, like Milton, imagined in 1652 that Cromwell would side against *hireling wolves*, i.e. the ministers of an Established Church, probably 'misconstrued Cromwell even then, and ought to have known his opinions better'.[2]

At the time when he wrote the sonnet Milton, who was aware of the 'odium of excessive praise',[3] no doubt sincerely admired Cromwell. One wonders whether Cromwell could have been absent from his mind when he wrote in 1656 to a former pupil, Richard Jones, warning him against excessive admiration of victorious princes : 'For why is it greatly to be wondered at if in the native land of wethers strong horns are born which can butt down cities and towns most powerfully ?'[4] That his final view of Cromwell was a disenchanted one has been urged by Smart (p. 92).

1 Cromwell . . . *men*] Masson described Cromwell's personal

[1] Though Milton hailed the Scots enthusiastically in 1641 in *Of Reformation* ('Go on both hand in hand O Nations never to be disunited . . .'), his attitude slowly changed. Sonnet XII and *New Forcers* betray impatience, the sonnet to Fairfax something more. In his *Observations* on Ormond's Articles of Peace (1649) and *First Defence* (1651) a fierce hatred of Presbyterian Scotland is apparent.
[2] Masson, *Life*, iv. 566–7, 613 ff.
[3] Cf. the Latin note prefixed to the complimentary verses in the 1645 volume.
[4] *Life Records*, iv. 115.

ascendancy at this time as follows :—Official business was conducted by Parliament and its Council of State, Cromwell being a member of both. "'The Lord-General", as he was called, was an authority by himself. . . . He was always named on every important Committee ; and very often a matter of difficulty was referred expressly to his judgment. Still, in a manner, he stood aloof. He was Lord General Cromwell, the commander-in-chief of all the forces of the Commonwealth, a vast independent power overshadowing and observing the government, rather than strictly contained by it' (*Life*, iv. 359–60).

1-2 *cloud . . . warr*] Cf. Virgil's *nubem belli* (*Aen.* x. 809) (Newton). *Cloud* is used as in Heb. xii. 1 : 'a cloud of witnesses'.

2 *detractions*] Royalist squibs against Cromwell abounded in the 1640's and 1650's, e.g. *A Hue and Cry after Cromwell* and *A Hymn to Cromwell* ('to the Tune of, Let Cromwels Nose alone'), both of 1649. Reflections on his appearance and character were all too common, as were puns on his name (pronounced *Crumwell*), as in the Royalist toast 'God send this crumb well down !' Parliamentary opponents of the Lord General added to these *detractions*: it was no exaggeration to call them a *cloud*.

3 *faith*] Alluding to Cromwell's well-known habit of searching his conscience in times of uncertainty : *faith* thus prepares for the importance of liberty of *conscience* (l. 13).

4 *peace and truth*] Biblical in origin : 'For there shall be peace and truth in my days' (Isa. xxxix. 8 ; cf. Esther ix. 30, Zech. viii. 19). The words might be used without any allusive intention, as in *On Time* and *Paradise Lost*, xi. 667, but the context makes this unlikely (cf. p. 146). *Truth* refers back to *detractions* (l. 2), as *peace* does to *war*.

5 *on the neck*] The neck, connected with the figurative use of a yoke, gave rise to various expressions implying subjugation

(*O.E.D.*), as in Joshua x. 24: 'Come near, put your feet upon the necks of these kings'.

crowned Fortune proud] An image deriving from Milton's 'malignity to kings' (Hurd). Having just lost his sight (early in 1652) and his wife (5 May 1652), Milton would not think kindly of Fortune.

6 *reard*] Because *a trophy* was originally a structure erected or set up (on the field of battle or in a public place).

his work pursu'd] To do 'the work of God' is a biblical commonplace, as in John vi. 28, 1 Cor. xvi. 10.

7 *While . . . imbru'd*] The Battle of Preston, 1648, which took place 'over the ground traversed by the Ribble and its tributaries' (one of which was the Darwen). Masson goes on: 'The stream [Darwen], and a bridge over it where there was hard fighting, are mentioned in Cromwell's own letter of 20 Aug. 1648, to Speaker Lenthall, describing the battle' (*Poetical Works*, iii. 291). The image was common in poetry: cf. T. Manley's *Veni; Vidi; Vici. The Triumphs of the Most Excellent & Illustrious, Oliver Cromwell* (1652), p. 38 —

> In little boats he sent a thousand foot,
> Over the Frith, to put the foe to rout.
> Who did so well, that the astonisht *flood*
> Was purple colour'd with the enemies blood.

9 Worsters *laureat wreath*] Cromwell's victory at Worcester (1651), like that at Dunbar (1650), occurred on 3 September. It finally killed all Royalist hopes, and, as Hurd observed, was described in Cromwell's famous phrase as his 'crowning mercy'.

10-11 *peace . . . warr*] Smart noticed the echo of Cicero, who compared the glories of war with those of peace: 'Vere autem si volumus judicare, multae res exstiterunt urbanae majores clarioresque, quam bellicae' (*De Officiis*, i. xxii). In the *Second Defence* Milton also urged that the victories of peace are superior to those of war (*C.M.* viii. 241).

M.S.—L

13-14　*paw . . . wolves*] The comparison of corrupt ministers
with wolves is biblical in origin (Acts xx. 29 : 'after my departing
shall grievous wolves enter in among you'). Milton often
employed it to stress the insatiable appetite of these *wolves* for
more *hire* — 'a pack of hungrie Churchwolves . . . following
the hot sent of double Livings and Pluralities' (*The Tenure of
Kings and Magistrates*, *C.M.* v. 58). Here *paw* stands for the
civil authority of an Established Church, the *civil sword* (for which
cf. *New Forcers*, l. 5 and note).

14　*maw*] stomach ; *hence* appetite, voracity. The end is an
anti-climax, thought Warton. Not for the poet, however, whose
horror of the *blind mouthes* (*Lycidas*, l. 119) of the established
clergy had become almost an obsession. 'What a plump endow-
ment to the many-benefice-gaping mouth of a Prelate, what a
relish it would give to his canary-sucking, and swan-eating
palat' he wrote in *Of Reformation* (*C.M.* iii i. 19), equating
pluralism and gluttony, and revealing his usual animus. Hatred
of the 'belly-cheer' of much-beneficed Anglicans was, of course,
common among the Puritans : cf. *Boanerges* ('the humble supplication of the Ministers of Scotland') (1624), where pluralists
living in 'pomp, state, glory, feasting' are denounced as 'deuour-
ing panches' (p. 9) ; and John Bastwick's *Letany* of 1637, which
attacked the 'delecacy, variety, and deliciousnes of their fare'
(p. 5).

XVII

TEXTS　(i) Cambridge MS., scribal copy [MS.] ; (ii) G. Sikes,
1662 [1662] ; (iii) Edward Phillips, 1694 [1694].

TITLE　To Sr Henry Vane the younger MS. *deleted* ; To Sir
HENRY VANE. 1694.

COLLATION

1   counsell] MS., 1662 ; counsells MS. *orig.* ; Councels 1694.

4   *Epeirot*] MS. (*orig.* Epeirote), 1662 ; *Epirote* 1694.

6   drift] MS. (*orig.* drifts), *etc.*
states,] 1662, 1694 ; states MS.

7   best, upheld] MS., 1662 ; best be upheld 1694.

8   Move by] MS. (*orig.* Move on), 1662 ; Mann'd by 1694.

10-11   Both . . . don.] 1662, MS. (Both . . . do<.) ; What
powre the Church & what the civill meanes / Thou teachest
best, which few have ever don MS. *orig.* ; Both spirituall powre
& civill, what [it meanes *deleted*] each meanes / Thou hast learnt
well, a praise which few have won MS. *second draft* ; Both
Spiritual and Civil, . . . What serves each, . . . 1694.

13   firme] MS., 1662 ; right MS. *orig.* ; Right 1694.

14   In . . . son] MS., 1662 ; And reckons thee in chief her
Eldest Son. 1694.

COMMENTARY

Sir Henry Vane the younger (1613–62), one of Milton's most
brilliant contemporaries, a statesman and amateur theologian,
resembled the poet in his attitude to some of the crucial questions
of the day and in his inflexibility in matters of principle. The
eldest son (cf. l. 14) in the large family of Sir Henry Vane the
elder (1589–1655), he was expected to follow his father in the
diplomatic service — his father being a privy councillor (1630)
and later treasurer of the household (1639) and secretary of state
(1640), a trusted servant of the king. But Vane the younger,
dissatisfied like Milton with the government and liturgy of the
Anglican church, emigrated to New England in 1635 to seek
freedom of worship, and in 1636 was there elected Governor of

the Massachusetts Bay Colony, though astonishingly *young in yeares*. Ousted from his governorship in 1637 he returned to England, became joint-treasurer of the navy (1639), then sole treasurer (1642–50) and a leading member of the navy committee till 1653, preparing the way for Blake's victories over the Dutch and giving outstanding service, to which Milton perhaps alludes in saying that no better senator *held the helme* at Rome. As a member of the House of Commons he soon became prominent in debate as an opponent of the court party, and his father also went over to the 'popular' side; as a lay member of the Assembly of Divines (from 1643 : cf. p. 35), and as one of the six English Commissioners sent to Scotland (1643), he found other opportunities to advance church reformation. On Pym's death (1643) he acted as one of the leaders of the Parliamentary party: together with Cromwell he advocated religious toleration, as later in 1652 when Milton appealed to the two men to resist the *hireling wolves* of an established church. Vane disapproved of the proceedings that led up to the king's death, and for ten weeks stayed away from Parliament. Nevertheless, immediately thereafter (1649) he joined the Council of State, or cabinet, and remained one of its most energetic officers till 1653, when his long friendship with Cromwell came to an end — for Vane denounced Cromwell's dissolution of the Long Parliament. During the Protectorate he retired into private life, suffering minor persecutions from Cromwell, and also one four-months' term of imprisonment designed to obstruct his election to Parliament. After Cromwell's death Vane, as one of the senior survivors, acquired influence once more in Parliament and elsewhere, but was unable to prevent the return of Charles II. Excepted from the Act of Indemnity (1660) he lay in prison for two years, and was then tried for treason, condemned, and executed in June 1662, impressing all bystanders with his fearlessness and dignity.

Of Vane's great ability little more need be said. Whenever

his own party was in power he found himself in the forefront of affairs; when he grew critical of Cromwell, his former colleagues took considerable pains to bring him round; and Charles II did not dare to let him live. One special gift of his, none the less, deserves some illustration, since Milton dwelt upon it: his subtlety in unfolding the drift, *hard to be spelld*, of undeclared or treacherous enemies. I quote two contemporaries, a friend and a foe.

Some of our Commissioners who had been with the King, pleaded in the House for a Concurrence with him. . . . But Sir *Henry Vane* so truly stated the matter of Fact relating to the Treaty, and so evidently discovered the Design and Deceit of the King's Answer, that he made it clear to us, that by it the Justice of our Cause was not asserted. . . .[1] He was indeed a man of extraordinary parts, a pleasant wit, a great understanding, which pierced into and discerned the purposes of other men with wonderful sagacity, whilst he had himself *vultum clausum*, that no man could make a guess of what he intended. He was of a temper not to be moved, and of rare dissimulation. . . .[2]

No wonder that the Cardinal de Retz wrote, after an interview with Vane in 1651: 'Vane seemed to me a man of astonishing ability (*d'une capacité surprenante*)',[3] and that Milton expressed respect for Vane's intellectual accomplishments, an accolade not carelessly offered by him.

Though the sonnet betrays no signs of a personal connection we may be sure that Milton and Vane knew each other well. Masson conjectured that Vane prompted Milton's appointment as Latin Secretary to the Council of State in 1649; whether or not this was so, Vane and Milton met frequently in the Council, and the younger man no doubt issued instructions to Milton on many occasions. They would be drawn together by common interests, their religion and politics and also their education —

[1] Edmund Ludlow, *Memoirs*, i. 268.
[2] Clarendon, *History of the Rebellion* (ed. 1826, Oxford, 8 vols.), iv. 291.
[3] J. Willcock, *Life of Sir Henry Vane the Younger* (1913), p. 221.

Milton despised most of the other members of the Council as mere men of action (cf. l. 11, note); and Milton seems in addition to have been friendly with Vane's younger brother Charles.[1] The events touched on in the octave of the sonnet probably brought about a special piece of collaboration by Vane and Milton, marking a triumph in the official career of both.

In the early years of the Commonwealth the Dutch had the largest merchant navy in Europe: even though Cromwell favoured a policy of alliance with Protestant states, England began to challenge Dutch supremacy on the seas — and the result was war. The Navigation Act (October 1651) limited Dutch imports to England; English fleets also plundered Dutch ships trading with France, since the French, though not openly at war, seized English vessels; and, thirdly, England claimed the sovereignty of the British seas, which the Dutch only acknowledged by striking to the English flag when themselves outnumbered. To try to settle their differences — or so they alleged — the Dutch sent over three ambassadors in December 1651. While these were still in England, Van Tromp and Blake exchanged broadsides in the Downs, both sides thought that provocation was given, and a fierce engagement followed. That was on 19 May. The Dutch immediately despatched a fourth Ambassador Extraordinary to London, Milton's friend Adrian Pauw,[2] to attempt conciliation and to press forward the treaty under discussion: he was received by Parliament on 11 June. The English Council of State had meanwhile (4 June) set up a committee to answer the Dutch, of which Vane seems to have been the most experienced member (he was President of the Council for the four-week period from 17 May to 14 June, he stood first in the list of names for the committee, and of course

---

[1] Masson, *Life*, iv. 80; French, *Life Records*, ii. 355.

[2] Milton complimented Pauw, 'the honour and the ornament of Holland', in his *Second Defence* (1654), and Toland mentions that Pauw 'particularly esteem'd' Milton (*Lives*, p. 160).

he specialised in naval and foreign affairs).¹ While the Dutch
continued to talk of peace through their ambassadors the Council
grew impatient, fearing that the Dutch, who were massing
together a large fleet and whose motives were indeed *hard to be
spelld*, had already decided for war and delayed their representatives in London only to assess the strength of the enemy. On
30 June the ambassadors finally received their passports. On 3
July, according to Sikes, Milton sent Vane his sonnet; and it is
likely that the English and Latin statements of the English case
against the Dutch, published on or before 9 July and in early
August, also came from his pen.²

Milton's special service at this time is recorded by his nephew
Edward Phillips.

Before the War broke forth between the States of *England* and the
Dutch, the *Hollanders* sent over three Embassadours in order to an
accommodation; but they returning *re infecta*, the *Dutch* sent away a
Plenipotentiary, to offer Peace upon much milder terms, or at least
to gain more time. But this *Plenipotentiary* could not make such
haste, but that the Parliament had procured a Copy of their Instructions
in *Holland*, which were delivered by our Author to his Kinsman that
was then with him, to Translate for the Council to view, before the
said *Plenipotentiary* had taken Shipping for *England*; an Answer to all
he had in Charge lay ready for him, before he made his publick entry
into *London*.³

Since Adrian Pauw arrived in London before Vane's term of
office as President of the Council expired we may assume that
Milton and his kinsman (John Phillips ?) submitted their trans-
lation to Vane himself, and that their speed helped Vane to
formulate his *sage counsell* and repel the Dutch. In short, the
sonnet perhaps derives from a particular conjunction in the lives
of the poet and the recipient.

¹ Vane's important rôle in the negotiations with the Dutch, even after the
end of his term as President of the Council, emerges also from the *Journals
of the House of Commons* (cf. vii. 139 ff.).
² Cf. *C.M.* xviii. 502; *Life Records*, iii. 229–33.   ³ *Lives*, p. 79.

Ten years after Milton wrote his sonnet Vane's biographer, Sikes, annotated it extensively — partly paraphrasing and partly enlarging upon Milton's words. I subjoin some extracts (from pp. 93–102).

The Character of this deceased Statesman [Vane] . . . I shall exhibite to you in a paper of Verses, composed by a learned Gentleman, and sent him, *July* 3. 1652. [Milton's poem follows]. In the former part of these verses, notice is taken of a kind of angelical intuitiveness and sagacity he was furnished with, for spying out and unridling the subdolous intentions of hollow-hearted States, however disguised with colourable pretexts of Friendship. This rendred him a choice Senator, an honourable Counsellour for publick safety.

. . . that he could conjecture and spel out the most reserved consults and secret drifts of forreign Councils against us, (which they reckoned as *tacita*, concealed till executed) the *Hollander* did experience to their cost.

The next branch of his publick usefulness in a political capacity, was his most happy dexterity at making the best of a war. Armies are to small purpose abroad, unlesse there be sage Counsel at home. He heartily laboured to prevent a War with *Holland*, but the sons of *Zerviah*, a Military party, (that too much turned War into a Trade) were too many for him, in that point. He therefore set himself to make the best of a War, for his Countries defence. . . .

This blessed Witness and Assertor of the Fundamental Rights, Truths, and Liberties of Christs Kingdom, as also of the Commonwealth of *England*, and that has sealed his Assertions in both kinds, with his blood, was not onely well skilled in setting the right bounds to civil and spiritual Power in the outward government of Worldly States, but he did yet more clossly (*sic*) distinguish between natural (whence civil springs) and spiritual Power. . . .

Sikes also gave his impression of Vane's character : 'He was . . . a most quiet calme, composed speaker forth of the words of Truth and soberness, at all seasons, upon all occasions, and in all companies' (p. 9) ; 'His gravity, purity and chastness of spirit was very exemplary' (p. 50).

The sonnet was written a fortnight or so after the death of John Milton *the younger*, the poet's *eldest son* (in fact, his only son), at the age of fifteen months (i.e. *young in yeares*). One wonders whether Vane's achievements brought to Milton's mind his hopes for his boy.

2 *Senatour*] Members of Parliament were called *senators* in scores of pamphlets of the time (e.g. Prynne's *The Antipathie of the English Lordly Prelacie* (1641), dedication; Milton's *Ready and Easy Way* (1660)). After *young in yeares* Milton probably plays on the derivation of *senator* from *senis*, old.

3 *helme*] Alluding to Vane's work for the navy. The 'ship of state' was a hackneyed metaphor.

gownes not armes,] Dedicating his father's *Essays in Divinity* 'To the Great Example of Honour and Devotion, Sʳ H. VANE Junior', early in 1652 (the year of Milton's sonnet), John Donne the younger paid Vane the same compliment: 'our Armies abroad depend more upon your advice, then upon their own force . . . they would prove but a Body without a Soul, if they were not animated as well as recruted by your Direction'.

3-4 *when . . . bold*] 'The firmness and policy of the Roman Senate, no less than the valour of its soldiers, defeated Pyrrhus, King of Epirus, and Hannibal. Cicero argues in a well-known passage in favour of civic virtues, as against those which are purely military, — *Parvi enim sunt foris arma, nisi est consilium domi;* and cites the dictum, *Cedant arma togae* (*De Officiis*, Bk. 1. xxii. 76)' (Smart). It should be noticed that Pyrrhus and Hannibal, having ravaged Italy, offered the Romans peace — just as the Dutch negotiated for peace in 1652 when they had already clashed with the English navy.

Milton probably recalled his sonnet when writing the *Second Defence*: 'Timoleon . . . than whom, a better man or more revered in the commonwealth no age has produced. Next, Appius Claudius, who, by nobly declaring his sentiments in the senate, delivered Italy from Pyrrhus, a formidable enemy' (*C.M.* viii. 65).

5 *settle peace*] Vane always tried to settle differences by negotia-
tion, where possible. As governor in Massachusetts he called
two opposing factions to a conference — one of which soon
after caused his own downfall. His greatest success was in
rephrasing the Solemn League and Covenant (1643) to the satisfaction of both the Scots and the English.

6 *drift*] meaning; plot. 'The deviation of a ship from its
course in consequence of currents' is another sense given by
O.E.D., a possibility here in view of Vane's naval associations
(but the first entry is dated 1671).

spelld] interpreted.

8-9 *her . . . her*] The poets usually imagine war as masculine
(cf. Shakespeare's *King John*, IV. iii. 149: 'Doth dogged war
bristle his angry crest'; *2 Henry IV*, Induction 13–14), but Milton
was perhaps influenced by Machiavelli's *la guerra* (cf. next note).

8 *two . . . Gold*] *Nerves* = sinews. In his Commonplace Book
Milton noted twice: 'Against riches Machiavelli argues soundly
that they are not the sinews of war as is generally believed', and
'Machiavelli denies that riches are the sinews of war, and refutes
the popular opinion about this matter' (*C.M.* xviii. 160, 212).
In the *Discorsi* (ii. 10) Machiavelli urged that 'I danari non sono
il *nervo* della guerra secondo che è la comune opinione' (Money
is not the sinews of war, as it is commonly supposed to be),
since 'la guerra si faceva col ferro e non con l' oro' (war is made
with iron, not with gold). Maurice Kelley has shown that these
notes of Milton should be tentatively dated November 1651–
February 1652, i.e. shortly before the composition of the sonnet
to Vane,[1] but the cliché may also have been brought to Milton's
mind by a *bon mot* of one of the Dutch ambassadors on 30 June

---

[1] 'Milton and Machiavelli's *Discorsi*' (*Studies in Bibliography* (1951–2), vol. 4).

1652: 'One of them remarked just before their departure: "The English are about to attack a mountain of gold; we are about to attack a mountain of iron"'.[1]

9-12 *besides . . . ow*] Cf. p. 158. 'The *civil sword* and the *spiritual sword* are common expressions in the books of the time, the sword being thought of under both designations as the symbol of authority, not as that of destruction and violence . . . The significance of spiritual authority was differently apprehended by different writers; but it was possible to speak of the *spiritual sword* in a purely emblematic fashion, without suggesting constraint or compulsion by any kind of force' (Smart). Milton perhaps alludes to Vane's part in the arranging of the Solemn League and Covenant: the English in 1643 desired a *civil* league, the Scots a *religious* covenant, and Vane succeeded in reconciling the two points of view.[2]

In his *The Retired Mans Meditations* (1655) Vane himself wrote a long chapter 'Concerning Magistracy, as in its primitive constitution and right exercise, it hath its place and beares its part in the Reigne and government of Christ over men, in this world'.

11 *which few have don*] In February 1652 Milton confided to Mylius his low opinion of the education of members of the Council of State: 'They were mechanics, soldiers, servants, strong and keen enough, but entirely ignorant of public political matters . . . Among the forty persons who were in the Council of State, there were not over three or four who had been outside England' (*Life Records*, iii. 164). Milton probably means that few other *senators*, or politicians, have studied the relationship of civil and spiritual authority, for the subject was of course much discussed by theologians, and in particular by the Assembly of Divines.

[1] *The Cambridge Modern History* (1906), iv. 471.
[2] *The Cambridge Modern History*, iv. 317.

12 *bounds*] boundaries.

13 *Therfore . . . leanes*] An image perhaps suggested by Milton's blindness. We read of at least one friend, Millington, 'who us'd to Lead him by the Hand when he went Abroad' (*Lives*, p. 275). Cf. p. 189.

14 *In peace*] Could mean 'peacefully' or 'in time of peace'. In the context the latter seems more likely, yet England was virtually at war when Milton wrote the sonnet.

eldest son] 'the *firstborn* of Religion, another trace of Biblical language. Cf. "Reuben, thou art my firstborn, my might, . . ." — Gen. xlix. 3' (Smart). Milton perhaps glances at such titles as Defender of the Faith, Most Christian King, etc.

XVIII

TEXT 1673.

TITLE *On the late Massacher in* Piemont. 1673.

COMMENTARY

The Vaudois or Valdenses, to whose misfortunes the sonnet refers, took their name from their founder, Pierre Valdes, a merchant of Lyons who taught the virtues of poverty and a simple Christian faith. Growing in numbers, they were excommunicated by the Church (1215), but, after spreading from Dauphiné into Lombardy and Bohemia, they were driven out of the cities and fertile regions by persecution, and their chief strongholds were groups of Alpine villages in France and Italy. On the Italian side they lived, in 1655, in the territories of the young Carlo Emanuele II, Duke of Savoy and Prince of Piedmont, whose government decided in that year to enforce an earlier treaty.

A peace concluded in 1561 between the Duke of that time and the Vaudois granted toleration to those of the 'heretics' dwelling in the valleys of the Pellice and the Angrogna, two tributaries of the Po, but excepted certain villages at the lower end of the Pellice valley. Into these villages the Vaudois had nevertheless infiltrated, and therefore an edict was published, in January 1655, ordering all those outside the agreed territorial boundaries to abandon their homes before three days elapsed, on pain of death. Ignoring various appeals and petitions from the unfortunate Vaudois, the government sent an army under the Marquis of Pianezza to enforce the edict. Little resistance was met. Pianezza then demanded quarters for his troops in the upper Pellice and Angrogna valleys, where the government had granted toleration. The Vaudois, though uneasy, allowed the troops into their territories. On 24 April a plan to extirpate the 'heretics' completely was put into execution: Pianezza's forces, Piedmontese, French and Irish, massacred the inhabitants, and gave vent to their religious feelings by committing the most shocking atrocities. Men, women and children were roasted alive, impaled on spikes, mutilated, hurled from precipices, etc., while Pianezza's soldiers also plundered and burnt down houses and churches. The survivors straggled across the Alps into France, where the Vaudois communities gave them shelter; many, however, died of exposure in the mountains. From France their leaders then called for aid from Protestant states.

None responded more feelingly or more energetically than England. Cromwell, the Lord Protector, 'was often heard to say, That it lay as near or rather nearer his heart than if it had concerned his nearest and dearest Relations in the World'.[1] A

---

[1] Samuel Morland, *The History of the Evangelical Churches of the Valleys of Piemont* (1658), p. 552.

collection, for the relief of the survivors, was arranged through-out England and Wales, and Cromwell's personal contribution of £2,000 was despatched at once. At the same time the Lord Protector wrote to the Duke of Savoy to urge him to end the persecution, as also to the King of France and to the Protestant powers of Europe, suggesting that they join England in repre-sentations to Savoy: these letters, composed by Milton, the Secretary for Foreign Tongues, share the indignation of the sonnet though not, of course, its exalted tone. Cromwell also sent to Savoy a Commissioner, Samuel Morland, who addressed a stern speech to the young Duke in Turin, and three years later commemorated his mission in a book about the massacre and related events (cf. note, p. 163). And Cromwell went even farther: he seriously contemplated landing an army at Nice and Villafranca, and was deterred only because the Duke made peace with the Vaudois on 18 August, and again accepted the principle of toleration.

For the most part I have followed Masson and Smart in out-lining the historical facts. Milton and his fellow-Londoners were kept informed more directly by the multitudinous news-letters of their age. It has never been observed, I believe, how closely the description and attitudes of the sonnet reproduce these contemporary accounts.[1] For weeks on end the subject was given great prominence: many of the extracts quoted below were reprinted within a few days in other publications, often *verbatim*. (I have made no attempt to trace the first use of a particular image or allusion, being concerned only to illustrate a general literary background. The italics are mine.)

The French, Savoy, and Irish and Savoy (*sic*) forces, were all joynt Actors through the instigation of the Priests and Jesuites . . . [who] gave them up to the Shambles. The *bloody* Butchers did not only drive them out of their dwellings and possessions, but forced some

[1] It is known, of course, that the news-letters reported the massacre: cf. J. M. French, *N. & Q.* (1962), ccvii. 59.

(which was mercy in comparison what (*sic*) they did to others) to wander up and down in desolate and *snowy Mountains*, without food or cloathing, where many were starved by cold and famine, Women great with child frozen to death, others newly delivered, and *Infants* hanging upon their dry breasts, Some were led to the tops of *Rocks* and Precipices, and their heads being tyed down between their legs, they were tumbled down . . . (*Perfect Diurnall*, No. 286, 28 May– 4 June. Elsewhere the last detail comes even nearer to Milton:) Others being naked were tyed neck and heels together, and *rowled down* from the tops of great Mountains . . . (*Weekly Post*, No. 231, 12–19 June. The picture of the *bones* that *lie scatter'd* draws on some such passage as:) there is scarce any thing now to be seen, but here a Head, and there a Body; here a Leg, and there an Arm; here a hand, and there a foot . . . (*ibid*. The Alpine echoes *redoubl'd to the Hills* were also mentioned:) But amongst so many furious assaults . . . did resound nothing else but the Cries, Lamentations, and fearful Scriechings, made yet more pitiful by the multitude of those Eccho's, which are in those Mountains and Rocks . . . (*ibid*.).

(Protestant reactions naturally became news as well.) From Holland they write, That most Protestant Princes and States are resolved to embrace the Cause of these persecuted *Saints*, and have declared their Resolution to joyn with the Protector of Great Britain to *avenge* their Quarrel . . . and to restore to their Native Countrey the poor banished men, who like the faithful *of old*, are wandring in the Wildernesses, . . . that they might sing as those that returned from the *Babylonian Captivity* . . . (*Faithful Scout*, June 8–15. The desire to *avenge* the *saints* was expressed by many Protestants. The officers of General Monk in Edinburgh sent him an address) concerning a *late Massacre* and cruell Murther [committed by those] drunk with the blood of the *Saints* [in Piedmont, promising to fight for the cause] *if the Lord shall make inquisition for that blood*, and call us or any of us to *avenge* the quarrell of his people there . . . (*Mercurius Politicus*, No. 262, 14–21 June. And Protestant sympathisers inevitably stressed the antiquity and purity of the Vaudois religion:) it will appear by good proofs, that they have retained among them the *purity* of the Gospel ever since the Apostles time . . . without any mixture of *Idolatry or Superstition* (*Perfect Diurnall*, No. 283, 7–14 May).

(In *A Collection or Narrative* by J. B. Stouppe, the Swiss minister who was a friend and correspondent of Milton, various incidents during the massacres described for the benefit of Cromwell were published at his command, a little later in 1655. Some of the passages quoted above are here reprinted, and there occurs also the commonplace found in the sonnet, l. 10:) the children of God are not lost when being massacred . . . we may find *in their bloud and ashes the seed of the Church* (p. 2).

Title] *Piemont* was a common spelling; *massacher* was also Milton's spelling in *P.L.* xi. 679.

1 etc. *Avenge*] Cf. 'And when he had opened the fifth seal, I saw under the altar the souls of them that were slain for the word of God, and for the testimony which they held: And they cried with a loud voice, saying, How long, O Lord, holy and true, dost thou not judge and avenge our blood on them that dwell on the earth' (Rev. vi. 9–10) (Smart). Cf. also Luke xviii. 7: 'And shall not God avenge his own elect, which cry day and night unto him . . . ?'

Saints] The Puritans were in the habit of calling true believers saints, following the Bible, e.g. Ps. cxvi. 15, Acts ix. 13: 'I have heard by many of this man, how much evil he hath done to thy saints at Jerusalem'.

1-2 *bones . . . scatter'd*] Cf. Ps. cxli. 7: 'Our bones are scattered at the grave's mouth . . .'.

2 *Alpine . . . cold*] From Fairfax's *Tasso*, bk. 13, st. 60: 'streams . . . / Distill'd from tops of *Alpine mountains cold*' (Warton).

3 *thy truth*] Cf. Ps. lxxxvi. 11: 'Teach me *thy way*, O Lord; I will walk in *thy truth*', and l. 13, note.

4 *Stocks and Stones*] A *stock* was a trunk or block of wood. The phrase *stocks and stones* often = 'gods of wood and stone' at this time (*O.E.D.*, citing Jer. iii. 9 : '[Israel] defiled the land, and committed adultery with stones and with stocks', etc.).

5   *thy book*] God's *book* is frequently referred to in the Old and New Testaments.   St. Paul wrote to the Philippians (iv. 3) that the names of his fellow-labourers 'are in the book of life'; cf. Rev. iii. 5 and v. 1 ff. : 'And I saw in the right hand of him that sat on the throne a book . . .'.

record] Cf. *P.L.* i. 361 ff. : the names of the fallen angels are rased from 'heav'nly Records now . . . from the Books of Life'.

6   *thy Sheep*] Not only an allusion to the biblical commonplace about God's sheep and the good shepherd : Milton also echoes the Psalmist's cry that the children of God must be prepared for persecution and slaughter : 'Yea, for thy sake are we killed all the day long; we are counted as sheep for the slaughter' (xliv. 22; cf. Rom. viii. 36).

Fold] an enclosed piece of ground, therefore an appropriate word for the Alpine valleys.

8-10   *Their . . . Heav'n*] Cf. Exod. ii. 23 : 'their cry came up unto God', and similar biblical expressions.

10-13   *Their . . . hunderd-fold*] Cf. Tertullian's aphorism that 'the blood of martyrs is the seed of the Church' (Todd). K. Svendsen also suggested the fusion of the story of Cadmus, who sowed the teeth of a dragon he had slain in the ground, from which armed men sprang up, with the parable of the sower (Matt. xiii. 3 ff.), some of whose seeds fell 'into good ground, and brought forth fruit, some an hundredfold . . .' (*Shakespeare Association Bulletin* (1945), xx. 155).

12   *The triple Tyrant*] i.e. the Pope, with his three-tiered crown,

M.S.—M

called *Tricoronifer* in Milton's Latin poem *In Quintum Novembris*, l. 55 (Masson).

13 *hunderd-fold*] *Hunderd* (= hundred) is a Miltonic spelling (*Arcades*, l. 22, etc.). The 1673 ed. reads *hunder'd-fold*.

thy way] Cf. l. 3, note, and Exod. xxxiii. 13, Ps. xxvii. 11 : 'Teach me thy way, O Lord . . .', etc.

14 *Early . . . wo*] The Church of Rome was regarded by the Puritans as the mystical Babylon of the Apocalypse, the doom of which was foretold (Rev. xvii. and xviii) (Masson). Smart added that Petrarch has several sonnets of invective against the papal court, which he identifies with the Babylon of the Apocalypse. In one of them, from which Milton quoted in *Of Reformation*, the papal Babylon is called 'Fontana di dolore' (cf. Milton's *wo*).

Milton may also have had in mind the prophecies of the destruction of Babylon in the Old Testament, with its various allusions to fleeing from Babylon (for which cf. further p. 165) : 'Remove out of the midst of Babylon . . . For, lo, I will raise and cause to come up against Babylon an assembly of great nations . . .', 'Flee out of the midst of Babylon, and deliver every man his soul : be not cut off in her iniquity' (Jer. l. and li. Cf. Isa. xlviii. etc.). *Babylonian wo* then suggests imminent wars in Italy — of which the Piedmontese attacks against the Vaudois could be thought a foretaste.

XIX

TEXT 1673.

COLLATION

7 day-labour] day labour 1673.

COMMENTARY

Milton scholars divide into two camps in discussing the date and mood of the poet's most celebrated personal sonnet. There are those who insist that the order of the sonnets is chronological and that XIX is therefore later than April–May 1655, the *terminus a quo* for XVIII (e.g. Grierson, Kelley, Miss Darbishire). Against them stands a body of equally distinguished specialists (e.g. Smart, Tillyard, Hughes, French), who prefer to date the poem in the period immediately following Milton's total loss of sight, early in 1652.

Smart, the closest of all students of Milton's sonnets, says that it was written in the early days of blindness; and the whole tone of it points that way. Milton believes that through blindness he is useless for his life's work ('that one Talent . . . lodg'd with me useless'). Could he possibly have uttered that belief after writing *Defensio Secunda* (1654) in spite of his blindness ? [1]

According to Tillyard, Milton in 1652 'thought himself help-less, unable to defend himself against the attacks he was certain would be made against him' : yet in 1654, when writing the *Second Defence*, Milton recovered his vitality and self-confidence and declared that

his blindness is less an affliction than a proof that God has marked him out like the great men of old, Timoleon the virtuous King of

[1] Tillyard, *Milton* (1930), p. 388 ; and cf. pp. 189-91.

Sicily, Appius Claudius the Roman Censor, for some remarkable work.[1]

To corroborate that the poet felt completely crushed in the early days of his blindness Tillyard quoted a passage from the *Pro Se Defensio*, where Milton comments on the appearance in England of the *Regii Sanguinis Clamor*:

The book was scarcely complete in sheets, before it was put into my hands in the council. Soon after that sitting, another copy is sent me by the person who was then president, accompanied with the intimation, that the commonwealth expected my services to stop the mouth of this importunate crier. But at that time, in an especial manner, I was oppressed with concerns of a far different nature. My health was infirm, I was mourning the recent loss of two relatives, the light had now utterly vanished from my eyes.[2]

I can see no evidence in this retrospect that Milton's blindness rendered him helpless. The Council certainly did not think so. And, as Masson pointed out long ago, it is a remarkable fact that in the seventeen months from December 1651 to April 1653 (a span including the first year of his blindness) Milton's 'diplomatic documentary work' greatly exceeded in quantity the similar work from his pen produced in the previous two years and nine months.[3] We should remember that Milton's eyes failed gradually over a period of eight years (1644–52), and that he would therefore have time to adjust himself to new working-habits. His activity for the Council suggests that he switched to his new life of 'total eclipse' fairly smoothly : had he been unable to do so the Council would surely have dispensed with him.

The loss of his sight in 1652 need not have implied a useless talent to a man as busy as Milton. It is also disputable that Milton discovered only in 1654 that his blindness might betoken the great man chosen by God for some remarkable work. As early as November 1651 he wrote or caused to be written 'I am

---

[1] Tillyard, pp. 193–4 ; cf. the *Second Defence* (*C.M.* viii. 65).
[2] *C.M.* ix. 13–15. [3] Masson, *Life*, iv. 486.

made perfect in weakness' in a friend's album, as again later in
1656,[1] a motto which suggests not the near-despair of the sonnet
but rather acceptance. The source of the quotation (2 Cor. xii.
9 ff.) will clarify; 'my strength is made perfect in weakness.
Most gladly therefore will I rather glory in my infirmities, that
the power of Christ may rest upon me'. Milton's observations
on this passage in the *Second Defence* explain the choice of his
motto in 1651, and compel us to reject Tillyard's reading of
Milton's mood at this time.

There is a way, and the Apostle is my authority, through weakness
to the greatest strength. May I be one of the weakest, provided only
in my weakness that immortal and better vigour be put forth with
greater effect. . . .[2]

If Tillyard's argument holds, that the sonnet expresses a situation
and a mood already conquered by the poet in 1655, we may
add that the same would be true in 1652 and 1651.

　　Neither 1652 nor 1655 seems to be a satisfactory date. Before
we consider a third possibility some obstacles barring our way
demand attention. The familiar title, 'On his Blindness', it must
be emphasized, carries no authority from the poet, but was first
printed, long after his death, by Newton, in 1752. Is the subject,
then, the presence or only the imminence of total blindness ?
The one chronological hint in the sonnet provides a clue.

'When I consider how my light *is* spent, e're half my days.' *Is*, not
was: he is referring to the time of writing. In 1652 Milton was
forty-three years old. To refer to this age as less than half his days
is optimistic enough; but to refer to it thus in 1655 when he was
forty-six is outrageous.[3]

But, one must retort, would it really have been so much less
outrageous for Milton to say 'ere half my days' in 1652 ? The

---

[1] *Life Records*, iii. 104, iv. 118. W. R. Parker seems to have been the first
to notice the significance of this motto ('The Dates of Milton's Sonnets on
Blindness', *P.M.L.A.* (1958), lxxiii. 196–200).

[2] *C.M.* viii. 73.　　　　　　　　　　　　　[3] Tillyard, p. 388.

critics have taken great pains to explain away these inconvenient words.[1]   In a sonnet so intensely religious, however, one's instinct is to refer them to the Psalmist's 'three score years and ten' — by far the most natural explanation.

Where are we if we take 'ere half my days' literally as signifying 'ere half my three score years and ten' ?   At the very farthest we advance from Milton's birthday (9 December 1608) to the end of his thirty-fifth year or his thirty-*sixth* birthday (in 1644), observing, with Masson, 'Milton's habit of dating not from the current year of his age, but from the year which he had completed'.[2]   We arrive, as it turns out, at a critical juncture in Milton's affairs — which he described in a letter to Philaras dated 28 September 1654.

It is ten years, I think, more or less, since I felt my sight getting weak and dull, and at the same time my viscera generally out of sorts.   In the morning, if I began, as usual, to read anything, I felt my eyes at once thoroughly pained, and shrinking from the act of reading. . . . Not very long after, a darkness coming over the left part of my left eye (for that eye became clouded some years before the other) removed from my vision all objects situated on that side.[3]

It is a remarkable coincidence : just as Milton was about to complete 'half his days' he perceived that his vision grew weak and dull.[4]   Could it be that in the sonnet he said no more than this — that his power of vision (light) is worn out (spent), though not yet totally destroyed ?[5]

[1] Donald Dorian thought that they might 'mean working days' (*The Explicator* (1951), x. item 16);   W. R. Parker, that Milton reckoned his life expectancy from the fact that 'his own father lived to be at least eighty-four. . . . Half of eighty-four is the age that Milton reported to Mylius as the time of total blindness' (loc. cit.);   E. Saillens, that Milton refers to an 'immemorial popular belief' that man lives for a hundred years (*T.L.S.* (6 Oct. 1961), p. 672);   and J. T. Shawcross also argued for a hundred years, citing Isa. lxv. 20 (*N. & Q.* (1957), ccii. 442–6).

[2] *Poetical Works*, i. 118.   [3] *C.M.* xii. 67.

[4] Parker noticed the coincidence (loc. cit.).

[5] Cf. *O.E.D.*, light, 4 : power of vision, eyesight;   spend, 10 : to consume, employ, use superfluously, waste, squander.

Another coincidence worth pondering is that, whilst Milton's *Talent* was never in danger of becoming *useless* when he finally suffered total blindness, in 1652, if we may judge from the pressure of his official work, he withdrew from the world for several years just at the time when he first grew conscious of his failing sight, late in 1644. Between 1641 and 1644 he issued several tracts a year : between *Tetrachordon* and *Colasterion*, both apparently published on 4 March 1645, and *The Tenure of Kings and Magistrates* (1649), he chose to *hide* his *Talent*.[1]

Perhaps, then, Milton wrote his sonnet shortly before his birthday on 9 December 1644, when he could not foresee to what extent he might adjust himself to failing eye-sight. Why, in that case, did he omit it from the *Poems* of 1645 ? We have to remember the purpose of that collection — which was, as Masson[2] has proved beyond doubt, to rehabilitate Milton's name, mud-bespattered from the pamphlet-wars. Hence Milton reprinted Wotton's encomiastic letter and the verses and testimonials of his Italian friends, and selected a pointed motto from Virgil. Hence, again, he seems to have refrained from inserting sonnet XI, 'On the Detraction which followed upon my writing certain Treatises', if, as is possible, he had composed it before publishing the *Poems* (cf. p. 117) : it would have identified the poet with the fiery controversialist, the very thing he wished to play down. For a similar reason, I believe, he would have excluded sonnet XIX : anticipating that his enemies would make capital out of his impending blindness as a judgment of God, as they had already pounced on his other supposed infirmities (cf.

---

[1] Cf. also E. Sirluck, 'Milton's Idle Right Hand' (*J.E.G.P.* (1961), lx. 749 ff.). Milton's *Poems* were published after 4 March 1645 (Thomason dated his copy 2 January 1645-6), but, unlike the pamphlets, would not require research from the author, who could ask friends to help with copying and proof-reading : sonnet VIII was in fact copied into the Cambridge MS. by another hand. I suppose that *Tetrachordon* was completed in the autumn of 1644, and that *Colasterion* was written very hurriedly, or dictated, shortly afterwards.

[2] *Poetical Works*, i. 89 ff.

An Apology for Smectymnuus), he would prefer not to publicize the fact.[1]

The available evidence therefore suggests three possible dates for this sonnet, 1644, 1651–2 and 1655. Each one is open to objections : I find it very difficult to choose between them. What is certain is that each of the three must modify our picture of the poet, and our interpretation of the poem.[2]

An article by Fitzroy Pyle gives an excellent introduction to the sequence of ideas in the sonnet.

The octave assumed that ceaseless labour is demanded of all, that this alone is acceptable service, and is rewarded in accordance with results achieved: the sestet grants that ceaseless activity at God's bidding is acceptable (if performed without thought of spiritual gain), but enlarges the concept of service to include the ministration of those who though inactive are eagerly prepared for action when the call comes.[3]

2 *this . . . world*] A cliché in religious writings for 'this sinful world', as in Peter Sterry's *The Clouds in which Christ Comes* (1648), p. 49 ('this Dark World'), and Crashaw's epigram : 'The world's light shines, shine as it will, The world will love its Darkness still'.

3 *Talent*] Cf. Matt. xxv. 14 ff. Milton claims only a single talent — his literary talent (with a pun on the word). With this

---

[1] When Milton's blindness became known it was hailed as a judgment of God (cf. the *Second Defence*, *C.M.* viii. 67, and the opinion of Cyriack Skinner's aunt, quoted Masson, *Life*, iv. 530).

[2] Lysander Kemp has proposed a fourth date and interpretation, which has won little support (*Hopkins Review* (1952), vi. 80–3): that the sonnet was written before Milton's thirty-fifth birthday, *c.* 1642, and deals not with loss of sight but with loss of poetic inspiration.

[3] 'Milton's First Sonnet on his Blindness' (*R.E.S.* (1958), ix. 382 ff.). For other discussions cf. Eleanor G. Brown, *Milton's Blindness* (New York, 1934); Paul Goodman, *The Structure of Literature* (Chicago, 1954); J. T. Shawcross, 'Milton's Sonnet 19' (*N. & Q.* (1957), ccii. 442–6); R. L. Slakey in *E.L.H.* (1960), xxxvii. 122–30; Gossman and Whiting in *R.E.S.* (1961), xii. 364–70; P. R. Baumgartner in *S.P.* (1963), lx. 203–13.

a poet could earn immortality, therefore to *hide* it meant *death*.
In his *Letter to a Friend* (cf. p. 97) he had already shown how
deeply he was impressed by the command in the Gospel 'set out by
the terrible seizing of him that hid the talent'. The 'unprofitable
servant' suffers spiritual *death* in losing the kingdom of heaven.

4 *useless*] A pun on *use* = usury, interest (P. Drew).

6 *account*] Perhaps Milton associates the parable of the talents
with the similar one in Matt. xviii. 23 ff. : 'Therefore is the
kingdom of heaven likened unto a certain king, which would
take *account* of his servants. . . .' He seems always to have kept
his final account in mind. Cf. a significant passage in *An Apology
for Smectymnuus* : 'guifts of Gods imparting, which I boast not,
but thankfully acknowledge, and feare also lest at my certaine
account they be reckon'd to me many rather then few' (*C.M.*
III i. 282).

7 *day-labour*] labour for daily wages, or hired by the day
(*O.E.D.*). Milton asks whether God demands a full day's labour
from those without sight, and thus alludes to the parable of the
labourers in the vineyard (Matt. xx. 1 ff.), some of whom worked
for a full day, others for only part of a day.

8 *fondly*] foolishly.
patience] Christian patience, or faith in Providence, could be a
saintly virtue. Cf. Rev. xiv. 12, and Ps. xxxvii. 7 ff. : 'Rest in
the Lord, and wait patiently for him. . . . Cease from anger,
and forsake wrath : fret not thyself in any wise to do evil . . .
those that wait upon the Lord, they shall inherit the earth.'
prevent] forestall (praevenire) (Verity). Cf. also *O.E.D.*, prevent,
4. '*Theol.*, etc. To go before with spiritual guidance and help :
said of God, or of his grace anticipating human action or need.'

9 *murmur*] Biblical, as in Ps. cvi. 25, 1 Cor. x. 10.

9-10 *God . . . gifts*] It was a commonplace that man returns God's gifts. Cf. *On the Death of a fair Infant:* 'Think what a present thou to God hast sent, And render him with patience what he lent'.

10-11 *who . . . best*] Cf. *P.R.* iii. 194 : 'who best Can suffer, best can do'.

11 *yoak*] Cf. Matt. xi. 29–30 : 'Take my yoke upon you, and learn of me . . . For my yoke is easy, and my burden is light.'

12-14 *Thousands . . . waite*] Some think that Milton compares two classes of angels, the inferior orders that *post o're Land and Ocean* with God's messages, and the superior orders that never leave God's presence and enjoy the highest contemplative insight. This would make the end of the poem a triumphant one (H. F. Robins, 'Milton's First Sonnet On His Blindness', *R.E.S.* (1956), vii. 360 ff.; so Grierson, Hughes). Others suppose that Milton compares angels and men, since Protestant theologians did not follow Scholastic distinctions concerning the angels (Smart, Pyle, etc.). This, the traditional view, is the more likely one, though Milton was certainly familiar with Scholastic ideas, for he seems not to have taken the angelic categories too seriously : e.g. in *P.L.* iii. 645 ff. the seraph Uriel is one of those 'Who in Gods presence, *nearest to his Throne Stand* ready at command', and yet he also bears errands.

14 *waite*] 'Wait on the Lord' (Ps. xxvii. 14) is a phrase frequently found in the Bible. Milton may use *wait* = attend as a servant, to receive orders (*O.E.D.* 9), but its more common meaning, 'stay in expectation', is surely present too : he reverts to the labourers in the vineyard, some of whom had to wait for work 'standing idle in the marketplace'.

XX

TEXT 1673.

COMMENTARY

While he lived in his home in Petty France, Westminster (i.e.
1652–60), Milton was frequently visited, according to Edward
Phillips, 'by particular Friends' — including 'young *Laurence* (the
Son of him that was President of *Oliver's* Council) to whom
there is a Sonnet among the rest, in his Printed Poems'.[1] Smart
has argued, quite plausibly, that Edward Lawrence (1633–57),
the Lord President's eldest son, is indicated, and not Henry
Lawrence, the second son, as was previously assumed: Edward's
great promise as a boy and as a young man impressed contemporaries, he had friends in common with Milton, and would have
been thoroughly worthy of the poet's friendship. But Smart
was, perhaps, a little unkind to dismiss Henry as one whose
'tastes were not intellectual': the evidence suggesting this is very
slight.

Edward Phillips described Milton's new home in Petty France
as 'a pretty Garden-house . . . opening into St. *James's* Park'.
The Latin Secretary would have had to walk through the park
to Whitehall[2] — if walk he did — and the sonnet may therefore
allude to the park's 'dank fields'. On the other hand, we know
from Aubrey that the poet's 'exercise was chiefly walking', that
after dinner 'he used to walke 3 or 4 houres at a time', and from
a later biographer that 'after he was Blind he us'd a Swing for
Exercise'.[3] The Secretary's attendances at Whitehall will not
have stopped simply because 'the Fields are dank, and ways are

---

[1] *Lives*, p. 74.   [2] Masson, *Life*, iv. 421.   [3] *Lives*, pp. 6, 204.

mire', though clearly Milton's walks with Lawrence were dis-
continued. It is possible, therefore, that the sonnet belongs to
the period when Milton still walked for exercise, before 1652,
and was addressed to a precocious youth of eighteen or nineteen.
I mention this alternative because the date usually assigned to the
sonnet (1655–6) is based on the 'chronological principle' which,
it has been shown, is suspect.

Writing of Milton in the 1640's, Edward Phillips informs us
that once every three or four weeks he 'would drop into the
Society of some Young Sparks of his Acquaintance . . . with
these Gentlemen he would so far make bold with his Body, as
now and then to keep a Gawdy-day'.[1] From the invitations to
Lawrence and Skinner (XXI) we may deduce, I think, that
Milton's partiality for gaudy-days lasted for a considerable time.

But this sonnet, like the next one, is not a straightforward
invitation (cf. p. 52): uncomplicated as it now appears, it
glances in several ways at an argument by which the Puritans
were much agitated. What sort of recreation could a Christian
permit himself? The question, debated in many treatises,
divided the Puritans — some opposing all self-indulgence and
even the arts. Milton's more humane attitude emerges from
what has been called his reply to Prynne's *Histriomastix* — from
Comus. But the stricter Puritans were sufficiently strong to close
the theatres (1642), to ban Christmas festivities, and to throw
all 'delights' on to the defensive.

That *delights* were a crucial issue may be seen in representative
books like Baxter's *Treatise of Self-Denial* (1659) and *Christian
Directory* (1673). 'We may use the creatures for delight when
that delight itself is a means to fit us for the work of God' —
not otherwise. We may drink to quench thirst: but if there
is a 'delicious gust', drinking becomes sinful, while a 'feast' of
two hours or more is 'luxurious' and 'sensual'. 'Diverting

---

[1] *Lives*, p. 62.

company' and 'idle visitors' are condemned, since 'All Time is
precious; but the season is most precious; the present time is
the season to works of present necessity: and for others, they
have all their particular seasons, which must not be let slip'.

Inclined as they were to bracket energy and toil with virtue,[1]
many Puritans held the same views as Baxter — to meet which
Milton framed his 'invitation' very carefully. Since rigorists
allowed only 'seasonable recreation' and insisted on the most
profitable use of time, Milton's *feast* is related to the seasons and
is defended as the only form of *gain* in mid-winter. But, accepting the other side's terms of reference, he develops a different
viewpoint. 'Season' has a larger meaning for him; the 'profit-
motive' encourages him to welcome *delights*, as the most gainful
recreation. And he strikes at the very basis upon which rested
the whole rigorist edifice, its worship of industry, by citing
Christ, who approved of the untoiling *Lillie* (cf. *stand and waite*
in XIX. 14).

1 Lawrence . . . *Son*] Cf. Horace, *Odes*, i. 16: 'O matre
pulchra filia pulchrior' (Pattison). I am not entirely convinced
by Smart that *virtuous* is used in the Latin sense and denotes no
more than 'mental power and capacity, eminence of character':
cf. XV. 5, note. It is true, however, that Milton admired the
Lord President as a man 'of the first capacity, and polished by
liberal studies' (*Second Defence*, *C.M.* viii. 235), and that Edward
Lawrence, who became a Member of Parliament at twenty-
three, was thought *virtuous*, in the Latin sense, by contemporaries.

4 *Help . . . day*] Cf. Horace, *Odes*, ii. 7: 'morantem saepe
diem mero/fregi' (Pattison).

wast] Could = spend or pass (time), without any suggestion of
wastefulness. But here the suggestion is present, and the reader's

---

[1] Cf. R. H. Tawney, *Religion and the Rise of Capitalism* (ed. 1961), pp. 199, 230.

attitude to 'seasonable recreation' determines his interpretation of *wast*.

what] whatever.

6 Favonius] 'The allusion to *Favonius*, the west wind, whom Horace invokes in a famous invitation to enjoy the delights of springtime (*Odes* i. 4), is the clearest of many Horatian notes in this and the following sonnet' (Hughes).

re-inspire] Alluding to the Latin sense, the renewed blowing of the west wind upon the frozen earth.

7-8 *cloth . . . spun*] Cf. Matt. vi. 26-30 : 'Behold the fowls of the air : for they *sow* not, neither do they reap. . . . Consider the *lilies* of the field, how they grow ; they toil not, neither do they *spin*. . . . Wherefore, if God so *clothe* the grass of the field, which to day is, and to morrow is cast into the oven, shall he not much more clothe you . . . ?'

9 *What . . . choice*] In the *Lives* we read frequently of Milton's 'constant Frugality', his 'spare Diet', and of his being 'no Friend to sharp or strong Liquors'.[1] His grand-daughter later reported 'that he was very temperate in his eating and drinking, but what he had he always loved to have of the best'.[2] *Neat* (of food) = dainty, tasteful.

10 *Attick tast*] 'The feasts of the Athenians were proverbial for their frugality and simple refinement, — *light and choice*. Plato in the *Republic* . . . allows wine in moderation, and cheerful talk' (Smart).

13 *spare*] afford. Most of the editors thought that *spare* = forbear, but the more recent tendency is to relate sonnets XX and XXI, stressing that the drift of the two is the same. Cf. F. Neiman, 'Milton's *Sonnet XX*' (*P.M.L.A.* (1949), lxiv. 480 ff.), and Elizabeth Jackson : Milton wrote 'in an Horatian mood to

---

[1] *Lives*, pp. 31, 62, 194.　　　　[2] *C.M.* xviii. 391.

urge his young friend to share in judiciously chosen Horatian delights' (*P.M.L.A.* (1950), lxv. 328–9). J. A. W. Bennett has also suggested that the sonnet's closing lines derive from the *Disticha Catonis*, iii. 7:

> Interpone tuis interdum gaudia curis,
> Ut possis animo quemvis sufferre laborem.

J. C. Maxwell added that Bennett's discovery supports the reading of spare = afford.[1]

14 *unwise*] 'Seems to allude to the "wise man" whom both the ancient Epicureans and Stoics in different ways admired as exemplifying their philosophic creeds' (Hughes).

XXI

TEXTS   (i) Cambridge MS., scribal copy, lines 5–14 only [MS.]; (ii) 1673.

COLLATION

8   intend] 1673 ; intends MS.

COMMENTARY

Cyriack Skinner's *Grandsire* was Sir Edward Coke, Chief Justice of the King's Bench, the outstanding jurist of his age, 'whose Person in his life time was reverenced as an Oracle, and his Works (since his decease) cyted as Authentick Authorities, even by the Reverend Judges themselves'.[2] The son of Coke's

---

[1] Cf. *T.L.S.* (1963), 5 April (p. 233) and 26 April (p. 314); also 10 May (p. 341) and 17 May (p. 357).

[2] 'To the Reader' in Coke's *Certain Select Cases* (1659).

daughter Bridget, Skinner was baptised in the church of Barrow-on-Humber, on 18 November 1627, some time after the death of his father, William Skinner, son and heir of Sir Vincent Skinner of Thornton College in Lincolnshire.

It is thought that Skinner was one of Milton's pupils at his house in Aldersgate Street (1640–5).[1] He entered Lincoln's Inn in 1647, but is heard of from time to time in the circle of Milton's friends. Writing of the visitors at Milton's house in Petty France (1652–60), Edward Phillips mentioned as 'particular Friends that had a high esteem for him' Andrew Marvell, young Lawrence, Marchamont Needham, and 'above all, Mr. *Cyriak Skinner* whom he honoured with two Sonnets'.[2] We know, in addition, that in the spring of 1654 Skinner became a near neighbour of the poet,[3] and that Milton transferred a bond for £400 to his young admirer on the day before the public proclamation of Charles II in 1660, and at the same time withdrew 'into a place of retirement and abscondence', until the Act of Oblivion. There can be no doubt that Skinner took a risk in accepting his friend's bond — if only the risk of losing his money.[4]

Apart from his connection with Milton, Skinner is also interesting as a leading member of the Rota, a political debating club set up in 1659 by republican sympathisers, which gathered every night at a coffee-house. (Here, presumably, he would *drench* his thoughts with coffee, not with wine.) Other members included James Harrington, the author, and the antiquary John Aubrey, who recorded that the club's political discussions 'were the most ingenious and smart that ever I heard, or expect to hear, and bandied with great eagerness: the arguments in the

[1] Aubrey noted that 'Mr . . . Skinner' was Milton's 'disciple' (*Lives*, p. 7), and that he was 'scholar to John Milton' (Smart, p. 118).   [2] *Lives*, p. 74.
[3] Marvell wrote to Milton on 2 June 1654, that he was 'exceeding glad that Mr. Skinner is got near you' (Masson, *Life*, iv. 621–2).
[4] Masson, *Life*, v. 702–3 ; *Lives*, p. 74.

Parliament House were but flat to it'.[1] Acting as chairman for
the club's 'ingenious and smart' theorising, as he sometimes did,
Skinner must have had a marked speculative talent — to which
Milton alluded, smilingly, when he advised the younger man
not to lose himself for ever in *deep thoughts* about *what the Swede
intend and what the French.*

It is not easy to determine the dates of the two sonnets to
Skinner. Masson, quoting Marvell's letter of 2 June 1654,[2]
inferred from it 'the reappearance about Milton in Petty France
of his old pupil of the Aldersgate Street days'.[3] Yet it remains
possible that the member of Lincoln's Inn lived elsewhere in
London before 1654, and that he sometimes visited Milton
before becoming his near neighbour: the sonnet could therefore
belong to an earlier year. On the other hand, sonnet XXI
almost certainly preceded XXII (1655). Complimentary allusions to the parents or ancestors of persons addressed in the
sonnets are so frequent that the absence of any such courtesies
from XXII suggests that XXI was already composed.

The unpredictable intentions of *the Swede* and *the French* also
fail to date XXI. Smart thought that *the Swede* points to Charles
X, King of Sweden from 1654 to 1660, whose reign was 'a
rapid succession of military exploits'. But England was negotiat-
ing treaties with both Sweden and France a little earlier, in
1653–4, and both negotiations ran into difficulties.[4] *The Swede*
could refer to the Sweden of Queen Christina, and *the French*
to the slippery France of Mazarin before or after 1654.[5]

---

[1] Smart, p. 118; Masson, *Life*, v. 484 ff.   [2] Cf. p. 182, n. 3.
[3] Masson, *Life*, iv. 621–2.   [4] Ibid., 553 ff.
[5] Skinner would have an even more important place in the biography of
Milton than that outlined above if, as has been suggested by W. R. Parker and
Maurice Kelley, he was the author of the earliest or anonymous Life of Milton,
which Miss Darbishire ascribed to John Phillips (cf. *T.L.S.* (1957), 13 Sept. (p.
547) and 27 Dec. (p. 787)). The argument rests on similarities of handwriting.
But I am inclined to agree with R. W. Hunt, Keeper of Western Manuscripts
in the Bodleian Library, that the hands are not 'distinctive enough to allow

1 Cyriack] The name is spelt 'Syriack' (= Syrian) 'both on his father's monument and in the register of his birth'.[1] Milton perhaps alludes to the 'national' implications when he goes on to speak of the *Swede* and the *French*.

1-4 *whose . . . wrench*] 'Of all the long line of judges who have rendered England famous among the nations for the excellence and impartiality of the administration of justice the chief place has been unhesitatingly awarded to Coke' (The Earl of Birkenhead, *Fourteen English Judges* (1926)).

2 Themis] The Goddess of Justice.

3 *his volumes*] Coke's *Reports* and his *Institutes* were his most celebrated volumes.

4 *their Barr*] The bar, or barrier, marked off the immediate precinct of the judge's seat. Milton therefore compared Coke not with barristers wrenching the law for their clients, but with other judges.

5 *drench*] drown. Cf. XX. 10, 'with wine'.

7 *Let . . . pause*] Cf. the dedication of Thomas Moffet's *The Silkewormes* (1599) :

> Vouchsafe a while to lay thy taske aside,
> Let *Petrarke* sleep, giue rest to *Sacred Writte*,
> Or bowe, or string will breake, if euer tied,
> Some little pawse aideth the quickest witte . . .

8 *And . . . French*] Cf. Horace, *Odes*, ii. 11 :

> Quid bellicosus Cantaber, et Scythes,
> Hirpine Quincti, cogitet, Adria
> Divisus objecto, remittas
> Quaerere . . .
>
> (Newton)

one to make a positive statement about their identity on grounds of script' (*T.L.S.* (1957), 11 Oct., p. 609).

[1] C. W. James, *Chief Justice Coke His Family & Descendants* (1929), p. 70.

Horace urges his friend to disregard international affairs, to remember that youth flies away and not to strain his mind trying to grasp the counsels of eternity.

9-10 *To . . . way*] One of the subjects studied by Milton's pupils (and therefore, presumably, by Skinner) was geometry. Their text-book was by Peter Ryff (*Lives*, p. 61). After the allusions to Euclid and Archimedes Milton turns from plane geometry, or 'the science of measuring', to other forms of measuring. ('Quid est Geometria ? Geometria est scientia (siue ars) bene metiendi'.) *To measure . . . the nearest way* perhaps glances at the proposition 'Si linea sit recta, erit quoque brevissima intra eosdem terminos',[1] and *solid good* at solid geometry. There is a similar association of ideas in *P.L.* viii. 82 ff., where Raphael laughs at astronomers who 'gird the Sphear With Centric and Eccentric scribl'd o're' and fail to appreciate the *solid good* (l. 93) close at hand. And again in the *Pro Se Defensio*, where Milton ridicules Vlaccus's pretensions to have advanced trigonometry : 'your creditors suffer for . . . your craft; and with them, it was incumbent upon you to conduct yourself, not as a trigono-metrician, but as a fraudless tetragonist; not to have been a measurer only of angles and obliquities, but to have measured out and rendered to every man his own (*oportuit . . . non angulos & obliquitates, sed suum cuique metiri ac reddere*)' (*C.M.* ix. 71).

14 *cheerful*] With a quibble on 'good cheer' ?

---

[1] Ryff's *Quaestiones Geometricae* (ed. 1665), pp. 9, 71.

XXII

TEXTS   (i) Cambridge MS., scribal copy [MS.]; (ii) 1694.

TITLE   To Mr. *CYRIAC SKINNER* Upon his Blindness. 1694.

COLLATION

3   light] MS.; Sight 1694.

4   sight] MS.; day 1694.

5   Of] MS.; Or 1694.

7   heavns] MS. (*orig.* Gods), 1694.

a] MS.; one 1694.

8   bear . . . steer] MS. (*orig.* attend to steer), 1694.

9   Right onward] MS. (*orig.* Vphillward), 1694.

12   talks] MS.; rings 1694.

13   the] MS.; this 1694.

14   better] MS.; other 1694.

COMMENTARY

Several recent critics think that this sonnet 'was apparently written on the anniversary of the day on which Milton had been forced to realise that his blindness was total, three years earlier'.[1] Smart, however, held that *this three years day* signified simply 'for three years', and compared *2 Henry VI*, II. i. 2: 'I saw not better sport these seven years' day'. Heywood's *Proverbs and*

[1] Nicolson, *John Milton*, p. 155.

Epigrams confirm this reading: 'This twenty yeres daie in weather hot or coole, Thou handledst no caruyng nor woorkyng toole'.

Though a 'year-day' or 'year's-day' was an anniversary, Smart must be right. Nevertheless it is not very likely that Milton would have used the phrase as late as the winter of 1655, when the fourth anniversary of his blindness was approaching. This has a bearing on the 'order' of the sonnets, for XX is an autumn or winter poem: cf. p. 61.

1-2 Cyriack . . . *spot*] That Milton was a handsome man is attested by several contemporaries. Cf. Manso's distich, and the anonymous biographer — who agreed, however, 'that his Eyes were none of the quickest. But his blindness, which proceeded from a Gutta Serena, added no further blemish to them' (*Lives*, p. 32). Milton himself insisted on this point in the *Second Defence*, since it had been alleged in the *Regii Sanguinis Clamor* (1652) that he was hideously ugly: 'to external appearance' his eyes 'are as completely without injury, as clear and bright, without the semblance of a cloud, as the eyes of those whose sight is the most perfect' (*C.M.* viii. 61).

4-6 *Nor . . . woman*] Orbs no doubt suggested *Sun or Moon or Starre*. Cf. also *P.L.* iii. 40 ff.:

> Thus with the Year
> Seasons return, but not to me returns
> Day, or the sweet approach of Ev'n or Morn,
> Or sight of vernal bloom, . . .

7 *hand . . . will*] God's *will* here = His purposes and commands (Matt. vii. 21), and God's *hand* = *either* His executive power (as in Acts iv. 30: 'By stretching forth thine hand to heal') *or* His chastisement (as in 1 Sam. v. 6: 'But the hand of the Lord was heavy upon them').

7-9 *nor . . . onward*] In a letter to Henry Oldenburg of 6 July 1654, Milton said that having vindicated Liberty he would prepare himself for 'other labours . . . An idle ease has never had charms for me' (*C.M.* xii. 65). Cf. also Job xvii. 9 : 'The righteous also shall hold on his way' ; Luke ix. 62 : 'No man, having put his hand to the plough, and looking back, is fit for the kingdom of God'.

7 *bate a jot*] deduct the least little bit. Cf. *Coriolanus*, ii. ii. 138-9 : 'neither will they bate One jot of ceremony'.

8 *heart*] courage.

bear vp] 'nautical term, used metaphorically. Cf. *Othello*, "A Turkish fleet, and bearing up to Cyprus". This is clearly, from what follows, the sense here' (Moody).

9 *★Vphillward*] Formed on the analogy of 'to God-ward' (Exod. xviii. 19), 'to thee-ward' (1 Sam. xix. 4), etc.

10-11 *The . . . task*] Cf. the *Second Defence* : 'when that office against the royal defence was publicly assigned me . . . my physicians expressly foretold, that if I undertook the task, I should in a short time lose both [eyes]' (*C.M.* viii. 68-9).

10 *conscience*] consciousness. Cf. Milton's similar statement, about his writing of the *First Defence* and his loss of sight, in the *Second Defence* : 'I would not exchange my own consciousness (*conscientiam*) of what I have done, for any act of theirs however well performed, or lose the recollection of it, which is always so calm and delighful to me' (*C.M.* viii. 71). John Toland tells us that Milton 'us'd frequently to tell those about him the intire Satisfaction of his Mind, that he had constantly imploy'd his Strength and Faculties in the defence of Liberty' (*Lives*, p. 194).

12 *Of . . . side*] Cf. the *Second Defence* : 'I now feel myself not in the forum or on the rostrum, surrounded by a single people only, whether Roman or Athenian, but, as it were, by listening Europe' (*C.M.* viii. 13). Morus ridiculed Milton for the prodigious self-esteem in his pamphlets (Masson, *Life*, v. 160); W. R. Parker has now urged (too vigorously, I think) that the biographers, following Milton, exaggerated the effect of the *First Defence*, that the *Second Defence* had an even smaller impact, and that Milton must have known by 1655 'that Europe no longer talked of him "from side to side"' (*Milton's Contemporary Reputation* (Columbus, 1940), pp. 35–8).

talks] The *rings* of 1694 was probably an unconscious transference from XV. 1: 'Fairfax, whose name in arms through Europe rings' (Smart).

13 *mask*] masquerade. Bacon also thought of the world as a masquerade — 'the Masques, and Mummeries, and Triumphs of the world' (*Essays*: Of Truth) — but Milton put more pressure on the word. We are reminded of the masks worn by masqueraders, by which their sight was restricted.

14 *Content . . . guide*] Cf. l. 10, note, and Milton's letter of 24 March 1656: 'I am glad, therefore, to know that you are assured of my tranquillity of spirit in this great affliction of loss of sight' (*C.M.* xii. 87). At the back of Milton's mind there is the thought that he, being *blind*, depended on *guides* to *lead* him. Perhaps Skinner sometimes *supported* the poet in this way. Cf. XVII. 13, note.

XXIII

TEXTS   (i) Cambridge MS., scribal fair copy [MS.] ; (ii) 1673.

COLLATION

13   enclin'd] 1673 ; enclin'd, MS.

COMMENTARY

The interpretation of various lines in this sonnet depends upon
the identity of the *late espoused Saint*.   Until recently it was
generally thought that Milton referred to his second wife,
Katherine Woodcock, who married him on 12 November 1656,
and who died on 3 February 1658.   W. R. Parker has shown
that this identification only goes back as far as 1725, and is not
supported by the early biographers: he suggested, therefore,
that Milton's first wife, Mary Powell (who died in 1652), should
be considered.[1]   Mary and Milton, he urged, lived together after
their reconciliation 'in good accord till her death', as several of
the early biographers testify ; in addition, they had four children.
We are not entitled to assume, with modern biographers, that
the marriage was not a happy one.   As regards Katherine, 'we
know nothing of her behaviour', and so the 'usual biographical
comments on her sweetness and goodness . . . are all inferences
from the sonnet'.   Parker then argued for Mary on two other
grounds.

(1) According to Lev. xii. 5, if a woman 'bear a maid child,
then she shall be unclean two weeks, as in her separation: and
she shall continue in the blood of her purifying threescore and
six days'.   Mary died three days after her daughter was born,

[1] 'Milton's Last Sonnet' (*R.E.S.* (1945), xxi. 235–8).

i.e. in childbirth; Katherine survived her daughter by three and a half months, i.e. she died after the period of purification, and, said Milton's grand-daughter, she 'did not die in childbed . . . [but] of a consumption'. 'Would not Milton have been more likely to think of "the old law"', Parker asked, 'if his wife had died *before* being "washed from spot of child-bed taint", and if he had later dreamed of her as still alive — as one who had, in other words, survived to be purified ?'

(2)   Of lines 7–8 Parker wrote that they 'cannot refer literally to Katherine Woodcock, because there is not the slightest reason for believing that Milton ever saw his second wife before his blindness. If he never had "full sight" of her, he could not have it "once more".' On the other hand, he enjoyed 'full sight' of Mary before losing his sight in 1652.

Parker himself and others pressed the case for Mary Powell in later articles, and Katherine Woodcock has also been vigorously defended. The arguments are not easily summarised: I shall select and compress rather drastically, leaving it to the reader to pursue the subject in the periodicals if he is so inclined.[1]

(1)   J. T. Shawcross (1956) agreed with Parker, asking why Milton laid such stress on his wife's purity. 'The reason . . . is that Milton wanted to contrast the purity of his wife's mind with the impurity of her body . . . The reason for impurity was that the necessary time-lapse . . . for purification after child-birth had not been fulfilled.'

I am not convinced. If the dead wife was 'as (one) whom purification did save', this suggests that the sixty-six days have passed (Pyle, 1949; Frye, 1949). The idea of purity could have

[1] J. T. Shawcross gives a useful list of nine articles, with very brief summaries, in *N. & Q.* (1956), cci. 202–4: (1) Parker (as above); (2) T. O. Mabbott, *N. & Q.* (1945), clxxxix. 239; (3) Fitzroy Pyle, *R.E.S.* (1949), xxv. 57–60; (4) R. M. Frye, *N. & Q.* (1949), cxciv. 321; (5) C. R. Dahlberg, ibid.; (6) Parker, *R.E.S.* (1951), ii. 147–52; (7) Pyle, ibid., pp. 152–4; (8) L. Spitzer, *Hopkins Review* (1951), pp. 16–25; (9) E. S. Le Comte, *N. & Q.* (1954), cxcix. 245–6. Add also T. Wheeler, *S.P.* (1961), lviii. 510–15.

been suggested by the *Alcestis* (l. 6, note), or by the epitaphs written for other women who died in or shortly after childbirth.[1]

(2) We may read lines 7–8, with their implication that Milton has *seen* his wife, since he hopes to see her *once more*, as referring to the glimpse of her in his dream (Pyle, 1949).

(3) Though Le Comte supplied several good reasons to explain why *Her face was vail'd*, I cannot resist the impression that one overriding reason determined this image. Smart stated it succinctly.

The allusion to a veiled face has been traced to a passage in the *Alcestis*; but in the tragedy Alcestis is not recognised by her husband when her face is covered, and is treated by him as a stranger until the veil is removed. Milton recognises his wife in spite of the veil. It is clear that he alludes to his blindness during their married life.[2]

As will have emerged, I prefer the old explanation that Katherine Woodcock was the *late espoused Saint*. Yet it would be folly to pretend that Mary Powell's claims have been completely disposed of. The sonnet, after all, could have been written before 1658.[3] Whichever view one finally takes it is worth while investigating the alternative, if only to learn that both are coherent in their different ways.[4]

[1] Cf. W. Cartwright's poem, 'On the Death of the most vertuous Gentlewoman, Mrs Ashford, who dyed in Child-bed': 'Her Body was so pure that Nature might / Have broke it into Forms . . .'.

[2] P. 125; cf. Parker (1951), p. 149; Pyle (1951), p. 154.

[3] It has been urged that Picard, the scribe who wrote out sonnet XXIII in the Cambridge MS., worked for Milton from 1658 to 1660, and that there is no evidence of any earlier connection between them. But, as Parker has said, Picard's version is a fair copy: the sonnet may have been composed much earlier.

[4] Leo Spitzer (1951) proposed an entirely different interpretation. He found it 'shocking' to imagine a particular wife as the *Saint*: Milton's subject, he thought, was the *donna angelicata* of Dante and Petrarch, a poet's vision of the Ideal. (Though the Renaissance 'tradition' contributed much to the poem (cf. p. 47), Spitzer surely underestimated the 'occasional' force of the sonnets: *spot of child-bed taint* identifies a particular wife (Katherine, or perhaps Mary), not the *donna angelicata*. For the same reason I cannot accept T. Wheeler's refinement of Spitzer that 'This is not Katherine Woodcock; it is an ideal in the mind of John Milton'.)

1 *Methought I saw*] Cf. p. 47.

late . . . Saint] 'can mean (a) "the saint whom I recently married", or (b) "the saint who was recently my wife", or (c) "my recently deceased wife, now a saint"' (Parker).

Saint] A soul in heaven. 'In one of the poems of Bembo, lamenting the death of his lady, he addresses her as *santa*' (Smart). Henry King, in *The Exequy*, published in 1657 but written long before, referred to his dead wife as 'my dead Saint'.

2 *like* Alcestis] 'In the tragedy of Euripides, one of Milton's favourite poets, Alcestis, wife of Admetus, gives her life as a ransom for that of her husband, and, after she has been borne to the grave, Hercules wrestles with Death and forces him to give up his prey, bringing back Alcestis alive to her husband. In a line which Milton follows, Hercules is addressed as "noble son of mighty Zeus"' (Smart).

5-6 *Mine . . . save*] Mine (came vested all in white), as one whom, washed from spot of child-bed taint, purification saved under the old Law. 'At the end of Euripides' tragedy we learn that, though Alcestis has been restored to her husband, subsequent purification will be necessary to release her from her consecration to the nether gods (*Alcestis*, 1144–6). The recollection of this may have helped Milton, dwelling on childbirth, to think of "purification"' (Pyle, 1949). Pyle later added (1951) that as the Feast of Purification fell on 2 February, 'the words "as whom . . . Purification in the old Law did save" refer specifically to the Virgin Mary, who, having survived "the days of her purification according to the law of Moses" (Luke ii. 22), was preserved. The image is a private one: if we did not know the date of Katherine Woodcock's death (3 February), we could not elucidate the lines.' Le Comte's reminder (1954) that the name Katherine comes from Gk. katharos (= pure) is also relevant.

9 *white*] Smart quoted Rev. vii. 13–14. Cf. also xix. 8 : 'And to her was granted that she should be arrayed in fine linen, clean and white : for the fine linen is the righteousness of saints'. Angels usually wear white in the Bible (e.g. Acts i. 10).

10 *vail'd*] Le Comte (1954) listed 'five logical reasons for "Her face was veiled"' : (1) Alcestis was veiled ; (2) if Katherine Woodcock is the wife referred to, Milton had never seen her ; (3) a veil would be appropriate for one of the saints in heaven ; (4) a veil would have been part of the dead woman's shroud ; (5) Milton may have thought of the 'churching of women', the ceremony of thanksgiving after childbirth in the Church of England : women had to be veiled for this. Le Comte concluded that the veiled face could not help with the identity question, as there were too many reasons for it : but cf. p. 192.

11 *Love . . . shin'd*] Milton may have had in mind a passage like Gal. v. 22 : 'the fruit of the Spirit is love, joy, peace, long-suffering, gentleness, goodness, . . .'

shin'd] Milton's usual form was *shone*, and he switched for the rhyme's sake. The Bible (Authorised Version) employed both forms, and is also responsible for the imagery of the shining face, which seems always to reflect heavenly goodness : cf. Ps. lxvii. 1 : 'God be merciful unto us, and bless us ; and cause his face to shine upon us', Eccles. viii. 1, Rev. i. 16.

13 *enclin'd*] The dream seems to melt into reality at this point : in the moment between sleeping and waking Milton is conscious of lying in his bed, and his dream lingers long enough for his *Saint* to appear to see him there.

14 *day . . . night*] Spitzer (cf. p. 191, n. 1) found the 'same paradoxical inversion of day and night' in a dream of the fifteenth-century poet Giovanni Pontano about his dead wife : 'At night, O wife, with thee I wander and thy shade accompanies me ; thus dark night for me is light and day ; but in day-light without thee I am rapt in darkness . . .'.

ON THE NEW FORCERS OF CONSCIENCE

TEXTS (i) Cambridge MS., scribal copy, much corrected [1] [MS.]; (ii) 1673.

TITLE On the forcers of Conscience. MS.; *On the new forcers of Conscience under the Long PARLIAMENT.* 1673.

COLLATION

1 of] 1673; off MS.

3 widdow'd] 1673, MS. (*orig.* vacant).

6 our] 1673, MS. (*orig.* the).

12 shallow] 1673, MS. (*orig.* hare braind).

14 packing] 1673; packings MS.

17 Clip . . . Ears] 1673, MS. (*orig.* Cropp yee as close as marginall P — s eares).

19 they] 1673, MS. (*orig.* you)

20 Large] 1673, MS. (*orig.* at large).

COMMENTARY

When it grew clear that the majority in the Westminster Assembly desired a Presbyterian settlement (cf. p. 35), Milton dreaded

---

[1] This scribal copy follows XVII in the MS., and so must have been written in or later than 1652, long after Milton first composed *New Forcers*. Therefore — though it is often forgotten — Milton's rejected readings were his 'final intention' for five years or more, and *New Forcers* might well be reprinted in this earlier form. Cf. also p. 103, n. 1.

two evils which had already done much harm under the protection of other Christian churches. He dissected them in later pamphlets.

Two things there be which have bin ever found working much mischief to the church of God, and the advancement of truth; force on the one side restraining, and hire on the other side corrupting the teachers thereof. Few ages have bin since the ascension of our Saviour, wherein the one of these two, or both together have not prevaild. . . .[1]

In the present sonnet Milton pithily indicates the dangers of force and hire: the civil sword will be used to compel consciences, and an established church will bring back pluralism. The sonnet to Cromwell rises to a climax on the same twin-themes, the fear that *secular chaines* will be imposed by the *paw* of *hireling wolves*.

The prelates had been *thrown of*, and the Liturgy *renounc'd*, in several stages — and Milton doubtlessly alludes to the general course of events rather than to particular occasions. The bishops were attacked before and after the first meeting of the Long Parliament (1640); in the Ordinance for the calling of the Assembly of Divines (1643) we read that the Lords and Commons have resolved 'That the present Church Government by Archbishops, Bishops . . . and other Ecclesiasticall Officers depending upon the Hierarchie, is evil . . . and that therfore . . . the same shal be taken away'; yet the Ordinance for the abolition of archbishops, bishops, etc., only came out on 9 October 1646. The Liturgy, the other chief target of Puritan attack, was finally renounced in the Ordinance forbidding further use of the Book of Common Prayer (1645), which was replaced by the Directory for Public Worship. By *stiff Vowes* may be meant the penalties prescribed (August 1645) for ministers who continued to follow the Book of Common Prayer: £5 for the first offence, £10 for the second, and one year's imprisonment for the third.

Milton naturally connected the attacks on prelates and on the

---

[1] *A Treatise of Civil Power*, 1659 (C.M. vi. 4).

Liturgy, as did all the reformers of the time : in some Smectymnuus pamphlets 'Liturgy' and 'Episcopacy' were bracketed on
the title-page as the two great causes, and the Assembly of
Divines was convened to consider these two subjects (church
government and form of worship). Nevertheless another implication should be explored. Archbishop Laud's name was sometimes made to pun with 'Lord',[1] and the Liturgy was popularly
associated with him — indeed, the rather similar Scottish version
imposed by Charles I was known as 'Laud's Liturgy'. It was
much remarked at the time that Parliament passed the Bill of
Attainder against Laud on 4 January 1645, 'the very same houre
that they voted down the Liturgy'.[2] A Laud-Lord pun therefore seems possible ('your Prelate *Laud . . . his* Liturgie'), the
more so because Milton had a weakness for playing with names [3]
and because it would lend point to the allusion to Prynne (l. 17).
Laud chastised Prynne before 1640 (Prynne was imprisoned,
pilloried, branded, lost his ears), then Prynne led the prosecution
against Laud (searching through his belongings, printing Laud's
diary with falsifications, and publishing various books against
him). The reminder that the *Civill Sword* was employed by
Laud against Prynne, and by Prynne against Laud, reinforces
the charge of mutual intolerance levelled by Milton against
Roman Catholics (*Trent, Priest*), Anglicans (*your Prelate Lord*)
and Presbyterians (*classic Hierarchy*).

This *charge*, and therefore the whole structure of ideas in the
sonnet, follows an Independent commonplace, which may be
illustrated from John Saltmarsh's *Groanes for Liberty* (1646) :

Did not the *Pope* whip the *Protestant* with *fines, imprisonments*, and
the *Prelate* take the rod out of his hand and whip the *Non-conformist*,

---

[1] E.g. by Milton's nephew John Phillips in *A Satyr Against Hypocrites* (1655),
p. 13 ('The Laud increase the number . . .').

[2] Prynne, *Canterburies Doome* (1646), sig. a₁ᵇ.

[3] E.g. Morus in the *Second Defence*, Marshall in *Tetrachordon* (Masson, *Life*,
iii. 311–12), Emilia or Francini in sonnet II (cf. pp. 77–81), and perhaps Bacon in
XI. 8 (cf. note).

and the *Non-conformist* or *Presbyter* take the same rod out of the *Prelates* hand and scourge those that are *Non-conformists* to him ? (p. 20).

The most likely date for *New Forcers* is early in 1646, since two of the Presbyterians referred to attacked Milton in print at about this time.[1] *Scotch what d'ye call* is now usually identified as Robert Baillie, one of the Scottish Commissioners in London (cf. p. 35), who summarised Milton's views on divorce in his *Dissuasive* (November 1645): 'Mr *Milton* . . . in a large Treatise hath pleaded for a full liberty for any man to put away his wife, when ever hee pleaseth . . .' (p. 116). Thomas Edwards in his *Gangraena* (February 1646) also named Milton as a divorcer. Masson suggested that Milton wrote his sonnet to punish these two Presbyterians. Smart disagreed.

It is unnecessary to imagine that Milton had such a motive. His interest in the controversy concerning Independence and Toleration is sufficient to explain the impulse which led him to write the verses: any other theory is gratuitous.[2]

Smart was right, I think, in seeing Toleration and Persecution as the poet's central interest. Yet for Milton, always inclined to generalise from his personal experience, being *nam'd and printed Hereticks*, his own recent fate, typified all that was most intolerant in Presbyterianism: Masson's reading is therefore quite close to Smart's. Indeed, the deleted allusion in l. 17 to Prynne, who had denounced Milton's divorce tracts a little earlier,[3] gives some support to Masson's notion of a personal flyting, as does the sonnet's sarcastic tone, so similar to that of the personal passages in *Tetrachordon* and *Colasterion*.

Humorous or satirical sonnets were sometimes given a 'tail' by the Italians, consisting of a half-line and a couplet. Two or

[1] It could hardly be dated *before* 1646 since Milton appeals to Parliament as anti-Presbyterian, and the Independents only made their influence felt after January 1646 (Don M. Wolfe, *Milton in the Puritan Revolution* (1941), p. 278).

[2] Cf. Masson, *Life*, iii. 468 ; Smart, p. 131.

[3] In September 1644 (Masson, *Life*, iii. 298–9).

more tails could be employed in the *sonetto caudato*. The form was not familiar in English poetry, and Milton's self-consciousness in resorting to it perhaps emerges from the antithetically related ideas of 'clipping' and 'writing large'.

Title. PARLIAMENT] Milton usually wrote 'Parlament' (So MS., l. 15; X. 5).

3 *★vacant*] Lat. *vacua*, unmarried, single.

Pluralitie] Pluralism was one of the features of the Anglican church most fiercely attacked by the Puritans, and a bill against it was passed by the Commons on 7 January 1643. Yet, as Milton repeated several times, no sooner were the Anglican pluralists taken out of their way than the Presbyterians jumped 'some into two, some into three, of their best benefices' (*First Defence, C.M.* vii. 61). The whoredom of pluralism was a Puritan cliché: cf. *Of Pluralities and Nonresidency*, a pamphlet of 1641 — 'Bishops who being busied about secular affaires, do intrust their Vicars with their charge . . . imitate whores' (sig. B$_1$^{a}).

4 *abhor'd*] A quibble after *whore*, l. 3, as in *Othello*, IV. ii. 162–3 : 'I cannot say whore;/It does abhor me now I speak the word.'

5 *Civill Sword*] Cf. XVII. 10, note.

6 *our . . . free*] Cf. XI. 10, note.

7 *ride us*] Cf. *The Doctrine and Discipline of Divorce* : '[This] is by the hard rains of them that *sit us* wholly diverted and imbezzl'd from us' (*C.M.* III ii. 485, where *sit* is misspelt *fit*).

classic] From *classis*, a presbytery (cf. p. 36).

Hierarchy] The episcopal form of church government was known as 'the hierarchy' to Puritans. It was named thus in the Ordinance calling the Assembly of Divines (cf. p. 196), in the Ordinance abolishing episcopacy, and repeatedly in Milton's *Of Reformation* and *The Reason of Church Government*, often as a term of abuse. Milton therefore brackets Presbyterianism (*classic*) with episcopacy.

8 *meer* A.S.] Adam Stuart, a Scot who lived in London at this time and wrote against the Independents. 'Adam Stuart was not a prominent figure in London during his brief visit; and *mere A.S.* suggests that Milton did not know what name these initials represented' (Smart). Yet numerous books by and against Stuart were being published, and Todd has shown that his 'name was well known'. I think that Milton echoed the Independents' indignation that 'this one single simple *A.S.* now starts up by him himself, peremptorily to state, and determine the Questions, for the resolution whereof the Parliament thought the Assembly of Divines few enough' (*M.S. to A.S. With a Plea for Libertie of Conscience* (1644), p. 2) : cf. next note.

Rotherford] Samuel *Rutherfurd*, as he usually signed himself. But both MS. and 1673 spell *Rotherford*, and after *ride us* Milton may have wished to play an *ass* (A.S.) and *rother* (ox), especially since others had already read A.S. as *ass* ('None but he that hath *A.S.* as part of his name, would say so', *M.S. to A.S.*, p. 18). Rutherfurd, Professor of Divinity and later Principal at St. Andrews, sat in the Assembly of Divines as one of the Scottish Commissioners (cf. p. 35), and advocated Presbyterianism in *The Due Right of Presbyteries* (1645) and *The Divine Right of Church Government* (1646). Smart noted that in a later pamphlet (1649) Rutherfurd brought out perhaps the most elaborate defence of religious persecution to appear in a Protestant country : and Milton was no doubt aware in 1646 of the temper of this celebrated divine.

9-10 *Men . . . Paul*] Smart showed (p. 129) that even Presbyterians, such as Baillie and Adam Stuart, acknowledged the learning and holiness of the leading Independents.

10 Paul] Many Puritans felt 'that the canonized names . . . used *Stylo Romano*, Saint *Paul*, Saint *Matthew*, Saint *Mark*, &c. ought to be laid aside, except they will use it of all Saints, and why not as well Saint *Moses* . . . ?' (G. Gillespie, *Aarons Rod* (1646), p. 310). Like the reformers, Milton tended to drop the 'Saint' at this time, though not quite consistently. He refers to Paul because the Presbyterians cited Paul as a bitter enemy of false teachers and therefore of toleration (Edwards, *The First and Second Part of Gangraena* (third edition, 1646), sig. 2L$_3^b$: '*Paul* . . . wished they were cut off that troubled the Church, and would not give place to false Teachers . . . [and] was against all Tolerations'; T. Manton, *Meate Out of the Eater* (1647), p. 49: '*Paul* is every where most zealous against errours, there is never an Epistle of his but hath some what against them').

12 *shallow* Edwards] Thomas Edwards, a Puritan preacher in London. He attacked the Independents in his *Antapologia* (1644) and in his more famous *Gangraena* (1646 etc.), a survey of religious deviationists or sects, in which Milton was disparagingly mentioned as a 'divorcer'. To prepare his *Gangraena* Edwards had clearly dipped into an enormous number of books, without much effort at understanding them.

Scotch what d'ye call] Robert Baillie, the only one of the Scottish Commissioners who 'expressed himself with bitterness against the Independents'. In his *Dissuasive from the Errours of the Times* (1645) he freely used such terms as *heresy* and *heretics* (Smart).

George Gillespie, another Scottish Commissioner, was thought to have been Milton's target by some earlier commentators, perhaps rightly. He was sufficiently bitter about 'pernicious, God-provoking, Truth-defacing, Church ruinating, & State-shaking toleration' (*Wholsome Severity Reconciled* (1645), sig. A$_3^a$), wrote of sectaries as heretics, and strongly supported the Presbyterian campaign for the right to excommunicate (cf. p. 203).

Moody thought that 'his harsh northern name' (cf. XII. 9, note) prompted the phrase.

14 *packing*] plotting, fraudulent contriving. The intrigues at the Council of Trent (1545–63) had become notorious. In *A Vindication of the Answer* (1641) by Milton's ｛Smectymnuan friends, a pamphlet in which he himself may have had a small share (Masson, *Life*, ii. 255–6), the same phrase occurs : 'such packing . . . as perhaps worse was not at the Councell of Trent' (p. 82). Milton here seems to address the Westminster Assembly (a modern Council of Trent), which was, of course, partly a *political* arena for Presbyterians and Independents.

17 *Phylacteries*] 'little boxes containing quotations from the Mosaic law which were worn on the forehead by pious Jews. Their display was made a byword for hypocrisy by Christ's charge that the Pharisees made "broad their phylacteries" (Matt. xxiii. 5). The line — as D. C. Dorian [1] observes in *M.L.N.* (1941), lvi. 63 — is a threat to the Presbyterians even though Milton says that the opposition to them may *baulk* at (stop short of) cutting off their ears and so, by a principle of the Mosaic law, rendering them incapable of priesthood of any kind' (Hughes).

*marginall P — s eares] Alluding to the Puritan William Prynne, whose ears were cut off in 1634, as a punishment for reflections on the king and queen in his *Histriomastix* (1632). He was again sentenced to lose his ears in 1637. 'Legends proliferated about Prynne's ears. To the Puritans, a miracle had taken place : his ears had been cut off in 1634, but God had made them grow again. The Laudians were more prosaic in their explanation : the ears had been lightly cropped the first time . . .' In 1641 Prynne published his account of the barbarity of this second

---

[1] Dorian argued that Milton changed l. 17 because the 'substituted line afforded a more specific threat against the intolerant Presbyterians'.

amputation: the executioner cut one of the ears so close that he removed a piece of cheek as well, and cut Prynne deep in the neck (cf. William M. Lamont, *Marginall Prynne* (1963) p. 39).

Many contemporaries commented derisively on Prynne's crowded *margins*, where he cited his authorities in his scores of legal and theological books. Samuel Butler called him

> This grand Scripturient Paper-spiller,
> This endless, needless Margin-filler . . .

and Milton had laughed at 'the gout and dropsy of [Prynne's] big margent, litter'd and overlaid with crude and huddl'd quotations', and later identified Prynne as one 'whom ye may know by his wits lying ever beside him in the margent'.[1] For Milton kept his margins remarkably clear of documentation, and disliked the 'marginal' writing of Presbyterian controversialists — because it revealed their love of *authority*, and because it produced the inelegant and unreadable books of A.S., Rutherfurd, Edwards, Baillie, Prynne, etc. The antithesis to *marginall Prynne* and the Presbyterian cast of mind therefore comes in l. 19 — *they shall read this clearly*.

Why did Milton change the line about Prynne? Because, it is said, Prynne's sufferings seemed no matter for jest.[2] But there may have been another reason. Noted Presbyterian though he was, Prynne opposed his party's demands for full powers to excommunicate heretics, thinking that this would lead to '*Arbitrary, Tyrannicall, Papall Domineering* over the *Consciences*, the *spirituall Priviledges* of *Christians*' (Prynne, *Foure Serious Questions* (1645), sig. $A_1{}^a$). Challenged by fellow-Presbyterians for taking this essentially Independent attitude, he explained that he opposed *abuse* of the power of excommunication and wished to 'controle the Arbitrary, Tyrannicall usurpations of some *Independent Ministers*' (Prynne, *A Vindication* (October 1645), sig. $B_1{}^b$). Yet

---

[1] *Colasterion* (1645), and *The Likeliest Means to Remove Hirelings* (1659) (*C.M.* iv. 234-5, vi. 66).   [2] Cf. also p. 202, n.

his position was not unlike that of the Independents in that he feared abuse of authority: as Milton in his sonnet deplored an authoritarian gesture very like excommunication (l. 11: 'nam'd and printed *Hereticks*'), it will have occurred to him that in this particular Prynne should not be classed with the enemy.

19 *in . . . charge*] in the indictment that will be brought against you (Verity).

20 New . . . *Large*] *Presbyter* and *Priest* both derive from the same Greek word, the contracted form coming into English through French. Anti-Presbyterian writers at this time delighted in bracketing the two words, to imply that Presbyterian authoritarianism was just the same as that of the Roman Catholics, — as in I. L.'s *Plaine Truth without Feare or Flattery* (1647), p. 7 (margin): 'marke & tremble all yee Priests & Presbyterians'. Cf. also the Anglican cry against reformers in general that they wanted ' popes in every parish '.

INDEX

Aitzema, L. de, 146
Alexander the Great, 104–5
Alleyn, E., 131
Anonymous Biographer, The, 114, 183, 187
Aphthonius, 48
Archimedes, 185
Aubrey, J., 55, 98, 177, 182

Bacon, F. (Viscount St. Albans), 74, 88, 112, 189
Bacon, Mr Justice, 117, 197
Baillie, R., 35, 198, 200–1, 203
Barnfield, R., 89, 131
Baroni, L., 80
Bastwick, J., 152
Baumgartner, P. R., 174
Baxter, R., 108, 178–9
Bembo, P., 88, 193
Bennett, J. A. W., 181
Bible, The, 51, 64, 98–100, 106, 108–9, 119, 122, 136–7, 150–2, 162, 166–8, 171–2, 174–6, 179–80, 187–8, 190–1, 193–4, 202
Birkenhead, Earl of, 184
Blake, R. (Admiral), 154, 156
Boanerges, 152
Book of Common Prayer, 196
Boscobel, 147
Bradley, A. C., 73
Bradshaw, J., 149
Bridge, W., 36, 38, 145
Brooks and Hardy, 88–89, 106
Brown, E. G., 174
Browne, Sir T., 74
Bucer, M., 122
Butler, S., 203

Cambridge Modern History, The, 161
Campbell, L., 99

Campion, T., 127
Carew, T., 128
Carey, J., 76, 78
Carlo Emanuele II, 163–4
Cartwright, W., 128, 132, 192
Casella, 49, 68, 129, 132
Catullus, 123
Charles I, 37, 53, 101, 103, 111–12, 129, 139–41, 143, 147, 153–5, 197, 202
Charles II, 140, 148, 154–5, 182
Charles X (of Sweden), 183
Chaucer, G., 85
Cheke, Sir J., 68, 122, 125–6
Christina, Queen, 183
Cicero, 151, 159
Clanvowe, Sir T., 85–86, 89
Clarendon, Earl of, 155
Clarke, E. (Milton's granddaughter), 180, 191
Coke, Sir E., 44, 49, 181, 184
Collcitto, 124
Collection of Epitaphs, A, 46
Collinge, N. E., 63
Constable, H., 39, 42, 107
Cowley, A., 96–98
Crashaw, R., 64, 174
Cromwell, O., 36–37, 72, 139, 145 ff., 154–5, 163–4, 166, 177. *See also under* Milton, Sonnet XVI

Dahlberg, C. R., 191
Daniel, S., 39, 108
Dante Alighieri, 68, 91, 113, 129, 132–3, 192
Darbishire, H., 55–56, 76, 89, 91, 107, 169, 183
Dati, C., 135
Davenant, Sir W., 128
Davis, Dr., 106

Declaration (of Scottish Parliament, 1648), 147
Della Casa, G., 40–41, 88, 108
Desportes, P., 48
Diekhoff, J. S., 132
Diodati, C., 76–78, 92, 96–97
Directory for Public Worship, 36, 196
Disticha Catonis, 181
Donne, J., 40, 64, 70, 74
Donne, J. (the younger), 159
Dorian, D., 76, 96, 99, 172, 202
Drew, P., 175

Edwards, T., 198, 201, 203
Englands Sole Remedy, 147
Euclid, 185
Euripides, 105, 141, 192–3
Evans, W. M., 127 ff.

Fairfax, Sir T., 37, 138 ff. *See also under* Milton, Sonnet XV
Faithful Scout, 165
Featley, D., 115
Fetherstone, H., 134
Finlay, J. H., 141
Fletcher, H. F., 54, 132
Fletcher, P., 137
Foss, E., 111
Francini, A., 79, 81, 197
French, J. M., 60, 100, 125, 143, 146, 149, 156–7, 161, 164, 169, 171
Frye, R. M., 191
Fuller, T., 111

Gardiner, Bishop, 125
Gill, A., 104
Gillespie, G., 35, 124, 201
Goode, W., 147
Goodman, P., 174
Goodwin, J., 102
Goodwin, T., 36, 38, 145
Gossman and Whiting, 174
Grand Army Remonstrance, 140
Grierson, Sir H. J. C., 137, 169, 176
Griffin, B., 39, 47
Groans of Kent, The, 147

H., I. (Gent.), 33
H., J., 123
Hanford, J. H., 54, 59 ff., 76–77, 80, 95, 103
Hardy, N., 116
Harrington, J., 182
Harvey, R., 50
Havens, R. D., 53
Henry, N. H., 120
Herbert, G., 64, 70
Herrick, R., 128
Heywood, J., 186
Hill, T., 32
Hobson, J., 110 ff.
Homer, 88, 136
Horace, 40, 52, 62 ff., 70–72, 74, 94, 123, 131, 141, 179–81, 184–5
Howard, Henry (Earl of Surrey), 39, 42
Howell, J., 77
Hue and Cry after Cromwell, A, 150
Hueffer, F., 42–43
Hughes, M. Y., 60–61, 92–94, 169, 176, 180–1, 202
Humble Proposals, 145
Hunt, R. W., 183
Hurd, R. (Bishop), 151
Hymn to Cromwell, A, 150

Isocrates, 113

Jackson, E., 180
James I, 111
James, C. W., 184
Johnson, S. (Dr.), 148
Jones, R., 149
Jonson, B., 39, 122, 131
Journals of the House of Commons, 31, 117, 124, 135, 142, 157
Juvenal, 98

Keightley, T., 81, 88, 91, 93, 136
Kelley, M., 58–62, 160, 169, 183
Kemp, L., 174
King, H., 193
Kuhl, E. P., 43, 91, 93

L., I., 204
Lamont, W. M., 203

Langley, C., 46
Laud, W. (Archbishop), 197, 202
Lawes, H., 54, 58, 68, 127 ff. *See also*
    under Milton, Sonnet XIII
Lawes, W., 127, 129
Lawrence, E., 52, 177 ff., 182. *See also*
    under Milton, Sonnet XX
Lawrence, H. (Lord President), 177,
    179
Lawrence, H., 177
Le Comte, E. S., 191–4
Lefkowitz, M., 127–8
Ley, J. (Earl of Marlborough), 49–50,
    110 ff.
Ley, Lady M., 49–50, 58, 110 ff. *See*
    also under Milton, Sonnet X
Lilburne, J., 119
Linche, R., 39, 48
Lodge, T., 39
Lok, H., 51
Ludlow, E., 103, 155
Ludwig, W., 63

Mabbott, T. O., 191
Machiavelli, 160
Manley, T., 151
Manso, J. B., 78, 187
Manton, T., 201
Maresca, T. E., 119
Martial, 50, 122
Marvell, A., 182–3
Massinger, P., 50, 137
Masson, D., 31, 33, 36, 50, 55, 60–61,
    70, 74, 76, 79–80, 103–4, 106, 111–12,
    115, 117, 123–4, 129–30, 132, 137,
    140, 142–3, 145, 148–51, 155–6, 164,
    167–8, 170, 172–4, 182–3, 189, 197–8,
    202
Maxwell, J. C., 181
Mazarin, J. (Cardinal), 183
Mercurius Politicus, 165
Meres, F., 39
Millington, 162
Milton, J. (Milton's father), 130, 172
MILTON, J., *Works*:
    Ad Patrem, 98
    Animadversions upon the Remonstrant's
        Defence, 120, 125

MILTON, J., *Works (contd.)*:
    Apology for Smectymnuus, An, 174,
        175
    Arcades, 130, 168
    Areopagitica, 33, 115, 120, 146
    Character of the Long Parliament,
        143
    Christian Doctrine, 135–6
    Colasterion, 114, 118–20, 173, 198,
        203
    Comus, 88, 98, 130, 178
    Doctrine and Discipline of Divorce,
        The, 107, 114–15, 121, 199
    Eikonoklastes, 53, 112, 148
    Elegies, 61, 70, 72, 76, 78, 80, 87–
        88, 92, 95
    Epigrams, 80
    Epitaphium Damonis, 78–79
    First Defence, 149, 188–9, 199
    In Quintum Novembris, 167
    Judgment of Martin Bucer, The, 32,
        114
    Letters, 79, 104, 188–9
    Letters of State, 54
    Letter to a Friend, 97–98, 175
    Likeliest Means to Remove Hirelings,
        The, 203
    Lycidas, 35, 152
    Nativity Ode, 61, 95, 98
    Observations (on Ormond's Articles
        of Peace), 149
    Of Reformation touching Church Dis-
        cipline, 149, 152, 168, 200
    On Shakespeare, 49, 98
    On the Death of a fair Infant, 176
    On Time, 150
    Paradise Lost, 33, 40, 71, 88, 93, 97–
        98, 100, 104, 120, 123, 137, 150
        166–7, 176, 185, 187
    Paradise Regained, 105, 125, 176
    Pro Se Defensio, 100, 170, 185
    Ready and Easy Way, The, 159
    Reason of Church Government, The,
        200
    Second Defence, 99, 100, 102, 118
        140, 149, 151, 156, 159–60, 169
        171, 174, 179, 187–9, 197
    Song on May Morning, 88

MILTON, J., *Works (contd.)*:
SONNETS:
I, 3, 46, 67, 69–71, 74, 81, 85 ff.
II, 4, 77, 89
III, 5, 77–79, 90
Canzone, 6, 77, 79, 81, 91
IV, 7, 77–78, 92
V, 8, 81, 93
VI, 9, 67, 94
VII, 10, 43–44, 46, 57, 67, 69–71, 77, 95 ff.
VIII, 11, 34, 69, 71, 74, 101 ff., 173
IX, 12, 44, 48–49, 57, 65, 69, 71, 74, 103, 105 ff.
X, 13, 41, 43, 48–50, 57, 65, 69, 71, 74, 103, 110 ff.
XI, 14, 32 ff., 43, 50, 57, 59–61, 65, 69, 71–72, 74–75, 113 ff., 142, 173, 197, 199
XII, 15, 34–35, 44, 50, 57, 59–61, 65, 67–68, 71–72, 74–75, 117, 121 ff., 149, 202
XIII, 16, 41, 43, 48–49, 54, 57, 67–69, 71–72, 117, 126 ff.
XIV, 17, 41, 46, 53, 57, 68–69, 117, 133 ff.
XV, 18, 31, 34 ff., 37, 43, 45, 48, 54, 57, 65, 69, 71, 74–75, 138 ff., 189
XVI, 19, 31, 34 ff., 38, 41–43, 45, 48, 54–55, 57, 62, 65, 71, 74–75, 142, 144 ff., 196
XVII, 20, 34 ff., 38, 43, 45, 48, 53–55, 57, 62, 65, 71, 74–75, 152 ff., 195, 199
XVIII, 21, 31, 38, 41, 43, 46, 59–61, 65–66, 71–72, 162 ff.
XIX, 22, 34, 41, 43–44, 46, 50 ff., 59–60, 62, 65–66, 70–71, 74, 169 ff., 179
XX, 23, 43–45, 52–53, 59, 61, 65–66, 71, 74, 87, 177 ff.
XXI, 24, 44–45, 52, 59, 65–66, 74, 181 ff.
XXII, 25, 43, 46, 54, 57, 61, 65–66, 70–71, 74–75, 183, 186 ff.
XXIII, 26, 44–48, 62, 66, 69–70, 74, 190 ff.

MILTON, J., *Works (contd.)*:
New Forcers, 27, 34–36, 38, 42, 50, 59, 74–75, 142, 149, 152, 195 ff.
Sonnets, Italian, 40, 57, 67, 74, 76 ff., 87
Tenure of Kings and Magistrates, Of the, 120, 148, 152, 173
Tetrachordon, 32, 44, 68, 75, 114, 118–19, 122–3, 125–6, 173, 197–8
Treatise of Civil Power, A, 136, 196
Milton, J. (Milton's son), 158–9
Milton, J. (Major), 143
Milton, *see also under* Clarke, E.; Powell, M.; Woodcock, K.
Moffet, T., 184
Monk, G. (General), 165
Moody, W. V., 102, 117, 123, 188, 202
More, A. (Morus), 189, 197
Morland, S., 163–4
Morse, C. J., 61
Moseley, H., 129
Mylius, H., 161

Nashe, T., 34
Needham, M., 148, 182
Neiman, F., 180
Nethercot, A. H., 97
Newton, T. (Bishop), 85, 124, 131, 150, 171, 184
Nicolson, M. H., 112, 118, 186
Nye, P., 36, 38, 145

Oldenburg, H., 188
Ovid, 104, 118, 131
Owen, J., 145–6, 149

Palmer, H., 114
Parker, W. R., 60, 95–96, 111, 118, 129, 171–2, 183, 189, 190 ff.
Patterson, F. A., 89
Pattison, M., 70, 113, 118, 136, 179
Pauw, A., 156–7
Perfect Diurnall, 165
Petrarch, 39, 41, 45, 48, 70, 76, 87, 90–91, 93–94, 97, 168, 192
Pettet, E. C., 64

Philaras, L., 172
Phillips, E., 54–56, 104, 106, 110, 130–131, 157, 177–8, 182
Phillips, J., 55, 130, 157, 183, 197
Pianezza, Marquis of, 163
Picard, J., 192
Pindar, 99, 105
Plato, 93, 180
Plomer, H. R., 135
Pluralities and Nonresidency, Of, 199
Plutarch, 105
Pontano, G., 194
Porrino, G., 90
Powell, M. (Milton's first wife), 80, 107, 110, 114, 151, 190 ff.
Prince, F. T., 40, 43, 81, 94, 108
Prynne, W., 115, 159, 178, 197–8, 202–4
Puckering, Sir H. N., 55
Purves, J., 91
Puttenham, G., 45
Pym, J., 154
Pyle, F., 61, 66, 174, 176, 191 ff.

Quintilian, 48, 68, 124

Racovian Catechism, 145–6
Rajan, B., 33
Raleigh, Sir W. (d. 1618), 47, 100
Raleigh, Sir W. (d. 1922), 33, 52
Randolph, T., 96–97
Reeves, Mr Justice, 117
Regii Sanguinis Clamor, 170, 187
Retz, Cardinal de, 155
Reynolds, E., 135
Richardson, J., 41, 131
Robins, H. F., 176
Rota, B., 47
Rutherfurd, S., 35, 200, 203
Ryff, P., 185

S., A., *see under* Stuart
S., M., 200
Saillens, E., 172
Saltmarsh, J., 197
Salzilli, G., 79
Sandys, G., 128
Schultz, H., 125

Scobell, H., 142
Shakespeare, W., 39, 42, 48–49, 51, 55, 63–64, 70, 72, 74, 88, 98, 103, 109, 131, 160, 186, 188, 199
Shawcross, J. T., 56, 58, 95, 138, 172, 174, 191 ff.
Sidney, Sir P., 39, 42, 47–48
Sikes, G., 54, 157–8
Simpson, S., 36, 38, 145
Sirluck, E., 95, 173
Skinner, C., 44–45, 52, 174, 178, 181 ff., 186 ff. *See also under* Milton, Sonnets XXI, XXII
Slakey, R. L., 174
Smart, J. S., 31, 38, 40, 42–43, 45–47, 55, 60, 70, 75–81, 86, 90–93, 96, 105–6, 108, 110, 112–13, 115, 120, 123–5, 132, 134, 137, 140–1, 145, 149, 151, 159, 161–2, 164, 166, 168–9, 176–7, 179–80, 182–3, 186–7, 189, 192–3, 198, 200–1
Smith, R. M., 96
Smith, W., 39, 47
Spenser, E., 39, 92, 109
Spitzer, L., 191–2, 194
Sterne, L., 74
Sterry, P., 174
Stevens, D. H., 60
Stoehr, T., 41
Stouppe, J. B., 165
Stroup, T. B., 47
Stuart, A., 200, 203
Svendsen, K., 99, 167

Tasso, T., 45, 93, 113, 166
Tawney, R. H., 179
Taylor, F., 32
Tennyson, A., 73
Tertullian, 167
Thomason, C., 46, 134 ff. *See also under* Milton, Sonnet XIV
Thomason, E., 135
Thomason, G., 119, 134–5, 173
Tillyard, E. M. W., 60, 169–71
To all that love Peace and Truth, 147
Todd, H. J., 47, 70, 108, 137, 167, 200
Tofte, R., 107

Toland, J., 156, 188
Tolomei, C., 113

Urquhart, Sir T., 148

Valdes, P., 162
Valentine, T., 137
Vane, C., 156
Vane, Sir H. (the elder), 49, 153
Vane, Sir H. (the younger), 53, 146, 149, 153 ff. *See also under* Milton, Sonnet XVII
Van Tromp (Admiral), 156
Vaughan, H., 64
'Verax, T.', 142
Verity, A. W., 111, 125, 136, 175, 204
Vindication of the Answer, A, 202
Virgil, 63, 70, 93, 98, 150, 173
Vlaccus, A., 185

Waller, E., 128–9
Walton, I., 131
Warburton, W. (Bishop), 142

Ward, J., 32, 116
Warton, T., 81, 88, 98, 103, 105, 132, 136–7, 141, 152, 166
Watson, J. R., 63
Watts-Dunton, W. T., 42–43
Weekly Post, 165
Wheeler, T., 191–2
Whitelocke, B., 124
Whitelocke, Sir J., 111
Wickham, E. C., 62
Wilkinson, L. P., 62
Willcock, J., 146, 155
Wilson, J., 127–8
Wolfe, D. M., 198
Wonderfull Deliverance, A, 102
Woodcock, K. (Milton's second wife), 190 ff.
Woodhouse, A. S. P., 76, 87, 95–96, 99
Wordsworth, W., 43
Wotton, Sir H., 173
Wright, B. A., 56, 107
Wright, W. A., 54–55
Wyatt, Sir T., 39

PRINTED BY R. & R. CLARK, LTD., EDINBURGH